RUTH
When God Leads Us Home

Richard Caldwell

KRESS
BIBLICAL
RESOURCES

Published by:
Kress Biblical Resources
www.kressbiblical.com

ISBN: 978-1-934952-42-9

DEDICATION

To the faithful believers who are Founders Baptist Church. Your faithful listening makes preaching a joyful labor.

CONTENTS

ACKNOWLEDGMENTS

I am thankful for the hard work that Nathan Ramirez devoted to this project. His editing of materials, and overall shaping of the project was invaluable.

INTRODUCTION

Ruth and Esther are the only two books in the Bible named after a woman. Both stories manifest the sovereign work of God in preserving his people. And in both cases He does this through the actions of faithful female protagonists acting on the plans of their wise parental figures. Even more intriguing than these common features are the contrastive details of the these two plots.

The book of Esther:
- is about a Jewish woman who marries a Gentile and is used by God to preserve the Jewish people through King Artaxerxes.
- never mentions the name of God.
- begins with a feast and ends with the death of 75,000 enemies of the Jews.

The book of Ruth:
- is about a Gentile woman who marries a Jew and is used by God to preserve the Jewish people through her great-grandson King David.
- is full of references to God, about 37 in all.
- begins with the death of 3 husbands and ends with the celebration of a birth.

These two unique pieces of our canon reveal the character of our God and are deep caverns of practical wisdom.

Purpose

The book of Ruth contributes to God's written revelation in three major areas.

- Genealogy – By supplying the heritage of King David it ultimately shows us the human lineage of the Messiah, King Jesus.

- Typology – In Boaz' love for Ruth and her love for him we have a picture of the relationship that Jesus Christ has with his church. This kinsmen redeemer illustrates the redemptive mission that Jesus carried out on behalf of mankind.

- Theology – Ruth is full of straightforward truths about God and his character. It intentionally magnifies the grace of God, the mercy of God, the patience of God, and especially the providence of God. It reveals God's absolute control over the lives of people and the forces of nature, and how he uses that control to quietly accomplish his purposes. His plans require neither human awareness nor human obedience to come to fruition.

Key words and themes

- Grace – God's grace may not seem like a key theme based on the number of mentions it receives, but when you consider how the book ends in comparison to how it began, you cannot miss it! Elimelech deserves to have his name forgotten after exchanging Israel for Moab, but God perpetuates his name and that of his son Mahlon through Obed. And as a native Moabitess, Ruth doesn't even deserve to be allowed in the community of Israel at all (Deut 23:3), but she ends up in the genealogy of the Jesus!

- *Ga'al/go'el (גָּאַל)*– to redeem/redeemer. Redemption is the buying back of something that has been sold. A redeemer is the one who pays the price for the redeemed to go free. Without a basic understanding of these terms, and the law of the kinsman redeemer as laid out in Deuteronomy 25 and Leviticus 25, one simply cannot comprehend either the plot or the significance of this book.

- *Chesed (חֶסֶד)* – This Hebrew word for loyal love is used to describe Ruth's love for her dead husband and for Naomi, Ruth's love for Boaz, and God's love for the dead (Elimelech, Mahlon, and Chilion) and the living (Ruth and Naomi). This is what makes Ruth the Moabitess a model Israelite: she imitates God's steadfast love in her various relationships. And God more than rewards her faithfulness by giving her the honor of bearing the forefather of both David the king and Jesus the Christ.

INTRODUCTION

Outline and Contents

There are many ways to outline the book of Ruth, but the two that prove most memorable and helpful focus on Ruth's actions and location.

Actions:
Chapter 1 – Ruth weeping
Chapter 2 – Ruth working
Chapter 3 – Ruth waiting
Chapter 4 – Ruth wedding[1]

Location:
Chapter 1 – In the land of Moab
Chapter 2 – In the fields of Boaz
Chapter 3 – On the threshing floor of Boaz
Chapter 4 – In the heart and home of Boaz[2]

Most of these chapters are comprised of multiple sections, and when these sections are analyzed and summarized the following expository outline emerges.

Chapter 1:
  - 1-5 When leaving leads to loss
  - 6-22 When God leads us home
Chapter 2:
  - 1-3 The Providence of God
  - 4-16 A Divine Appointment
  - 17-23 Living in Hope
Chapter 3
  - 1-18 A Request for Marriage
Chapter 4
  - 1-10 The Kinsmen Redeemer
  - 11-12 The Redeemed Bride.
  - 13-22 Overwhelmed with Blessing

---

[1] Warren W. Wiersbe, *Be Committed*, "Be" Commentary Series (Wheaton, IL: Victor Books, 1993), 12.

[2] J. Vernon McGee, *Thru the Bible Commentary: History of Israel (Ruth)*, electronic ed., vol. 11 (Nashville: Thomas Nelson, 1991), xi.

Each of the nine movements listed above will be further developed in its corresponding chapter. This development will include both exegetical insights and practical modern applications. My goal is that it might become evident to you how this story speaks to your life and the lives of those around you. Until we take hold of the timeless implications of this book, we can never use it effectively as a tool for building up the Lord's people who so desperately need the message it contains.

1
WHEN LEAVING LEADS TO LOSS
(1:1-5)

There is a time when it is better to stay in the midst of your problems than to leave in the hope of a promise. There is a time when the safest place to be in the world is in the place where it seems like everything is falling apart, and the most dangerous place to be is in a place where everything seems calm. You know that you are in such a time when enduring equals abiding in God's will and departing equals straying from it. You are in such a time when the place of pain is a part of God's plan and the place of supposed promise requires departure from what would please Him. There are many people in this world and in the church who have never learned this lesson. They fear their circumstances more than they fear disobedience to God. They would rather leave His will and grieve Him for the promise of comfort than cleave to his will and please Him in the midst of suffering. We live among a generation of people who believe that running away is a way of solving problems, that the answer is to wander, move on, and find a different place in the hope that their troubles will not follow them there. In their thinking, if you have trouble in your marriage, what do you do? You run. If you have problems at your job, what do you do? You run. If there are difficulties in your friendships, what do you do? You run.

Can you imagine how different and deficient the legacy of God's people would be if they had all adopted this mindset? Just stop and think about how many people in the Bible could have disobeyed God by choosing ease over divinely appointed difficult circumstances. Think about Daniel. To stay out of trouble, Daniel could have compromised on his convictions, but he didn't do it. Think about the three Hebrew sons who ended up in the fiery furnace. They could have bowed down to the golden image and spared themselves great conflict, but instead they obeyed the Lord. Think about Moses. We read in Hebrews 11 that he could have chosen to be known as the son of Pharaoh's daughter, but instead he chose to be numbered among God's people and to suffer on behalf of Christ.

Clearly this is not a new temptation. In 1 Timothy 1:3, Paul says to Timothy: *as I urged you when I was going to Macedonia, remain at Ephesus so that you may charge certain persons not to teach any different doctrine.* Timothy was in a challenging place. His youth was being despised in his church. There were false teachers making inroads into the congregation. He was wrestling inwardly with his own insecure disposition. Who wouldn't want to get out of Ephesus and experience relief from such an uncomfortable position? Paul's counsel, however, did not change with this influx of obstacles. He says, in effect, "Stay put, Timothy. God has a job for you to do there." Ever since then, Christ's under-shepherds have continued to guard His people against this familiar tendency. Martin Luther set the example for millions of saints over hundreds of years by taking a stand for the truth instead of bowing to the Pope's pressure. Matthew Henry echoed this theme in his day, declaring "it is seldom that changing our place is mending it.[3]" Warren Wiersbe warned that "you cannot leave behind what is the basic cause of most of our problems, an unbelieving and disobedient heart."[4] For modern church members to respond biblically to adversity, this timeless truth must resound from our pulpits as well, and few passages of Scripture present it as plainly as the first chapter of Ruth.

The Setting (1:1)
Time

Verse one tells us that these events take place during the time of the Judges. At this point in history, God's people had already wrested control of Canaan from its inhabitants but had not yet requested a king. It was a one of the darkest times in the history of the nation of Israel. Socially, it was a time of lawlessness. Rampant violence, crime, and restlessness gave birth to upheaval, unrest and warfare. Spiritually, the situation was equally debased. When the light of social righteousness dims, we can be sure that the light of spiritual truth faded first. Apathy gave way to immorality, which in turn yielded idolatry and ultimately apostasy. An abundance of corrupt leaders served as both a cause and an effect of this ethical degradation. For a summary statement of the cultural climate in the days of Ruth, simply examine the verse immediately preceding it, Judges 21:25. *In those days there was no king in Israel. Everyone did what was right in his own eyes.*

In the midst of this moral relativism, we are privileged to behold a

---

[3] Matthew Henry, *Commentary*, on Ruth 1:1-2
[4] Wiersbe, Warren, *Be Committed* (Elgin, IL: David C. Cook, 2008)

woman of true virtue. Refusing to live according to the spirit of the age, she staked her life on the truth and on the love of her God. The New Testament frequently calls believers to follow in the footsteps of the faithful saints who came before us, and we desperately need men and women who will walk in the way of Ruth. We need people who are not products of peer pressure, but powerful forces of conviction who aim to awaken the slumbering consciences of those surrounding them. We need believers who seek to impact and influence their world—not just with their lips, but with their faithful lives.

Trouble

As the crown of creation, humanity has always had an influential relationship with the earth. When Adam fell, the rest of physical creation plummeted with him, and to this day the earth remains cursed on account of man's sinful decision. Mankind is in rebellion to God and so, generally speaking, nature is in rebellion to man. This antagonistic relationship affects all people for all time to some degree, but for those living under the Mosaic covenant, the connection between man and nature was purposefully intensified. God established a direct, continuous causality between the submission of his people to him and the submission of the land to his people.

> But if you will not obey the voice of the LORD your God or be careful to do all his commandments and his statutes that I command you today, then all these curses shall come upon you and overtake you. Cursed shall you be in the city, and cursed shall you be in the field. Cursed shall be your basket and your kneading bowl. Cursed shall be the fruit of your womb and the fruit of your ground, the increase of your herds and the young of your flock… The LORD will strike you with wasting disease and with fever, inflammation and fiery heat, and with drought and with blight and with mildew… And the heavens over your head shall be bronze, and the earth under you shall be iron. The LORD will make the rain of your land powder. From heaven dust shall come down on you until you are destroyed… You shall carry much seed into the field and shall gather in little, for the locust shall consume it. You shall plant vineyards and dress them, but you shall neither drink of the wine nor gather the grapes, for the worm shall eat them. You shall have olive trees throughout all your territory, but you shall not anoint yourself with the oil, for your olives shall drop off… The cricket shall possess all your trees and the fruit of your ground.[5]

Considering these promised curses and the characteristic wickedness during the days of the Judges, it is not at all surprising to read that the Lord had gripped the land in the vise of famine.

---

[5] Deuteronomy 28:15-42

The Sojourn (1:2)
Ignoring their names
In the midst of this trouble, in the town of Bethlehem, lived the future father-in-law of Ruth, Elimelech, his wife Naomi, and their two sons, Mahlon and Chilion. At this point in the story the ancient Hebrew reader had an inherent advantage over those of us reading Ruth from a translation. As is often the case in Old Testament narrative, the meaning of the names adorns the account with irony and foreshadowing.

The irony begins with the notion of a famine in Bethlehem or the 'house of bread,' so named for the grain fields which encircled it. What was normally a place of provision and fertility was reduced to barrenness under the heavy hand of God. The wordplay continues with the mention of Elimelech, (my God is king) and his wife Naomi (sweet). A man whose very name denotes the authority of God ought to trust in and turn to God in times of trouble, as opposed to seeking shelter in the fields of God's enemies. This woman whose name drips sweetness is about to taste the bitterness of her husband's sinful choice. It is also possible that Naomi is an abbreviation of a theophoric name which would have had the full meaning 'God is sweet.' If this is the case, then the author masterfully foreshadows the theological agenda of the book in its opening lines. The book's prominent concern is to highlight God's sovereignty over everything and his goodness toward his people. What better way to capture this message than to subtly reveal that God is a sweet king? When we consider that these names were not imagined by the human author, but announced by unassuming parents decades before the events of Ruth took place, we begin to worship the sovereign goodness of God at work through the providential naming of these lowly Bethlehemites.

If Elimelech had lived up to the faith of those who named him, the story might have ended here. Instead, he ignores the irony of it all and makes the sinful decision to move his family fifty miles east to the land of Moab. The presumed reason for relocation is that in Moab times were not as tough. In Moab there was the promise of bread. We have all known people, including faithful people, who moved with the express purpose of finding work, so what made this a wrong choice from the outset?

Forgetting who they were
It was a sinful sojourn because they forgot who they were. This was a family that was in covenant with God. They were a part of a chosen nation. They belonged to a people who had been divinely delivered from Egypt and then led by the commandment and the clear hand of God into the land of their inheritance. The Israelites were not in Canaan because they had chosen Canaan. They were in Canaan because this was the property that God had assigned to them. He led them to this place and established them in this place. He told them that this is where He wanted them to be. As a part of this

people, Elimelech had no right to leave the place where God had placed him just because the circumstances were tough. Instead, they should have sought God's blessing by seeking His face and encouraging their neighbors to do the same. Elimelech and Naomi forgot or ignored the fact that they did not belong to themselves. They were God's people, and they were to obey Him.

Do we realize that the same is true of us? We are in covenant with God through the blood of our savior. We are a part of a holy nation gathered from among all the nations of the world. We belong to a people who have been divinely delivered from the domain of darkness and transferred to the kingdom of God's beloved Son. Just as they were to abide in the <u>place</u> where God established them, so we are to abide in the <u>Person</u> through whom God rescued us. We are called to abide in Christ, regardless of the dangers that threaten us or the difficulties that impede us. If we are Christians, we cannot live as though God has no claim upon our lives, and then expect to abide in His blessing in terms of spiritual fruitfulness. In fact, when we begin to live this way, God will often bring circumstances to bear upon our lives to awaken us from the delusion of self-autonomy and remind us of who we really are.

Disregarding what God said

It was a sinful sojourn because they ignored what God clearly commanded. They had enough information from God to know that this move was contrary to His revealed will. Listen to the Law's discrimination against the Moabites in Deuteronomy 23:3-6.

> No *Ammonite or Moabite may enter the assembly of the* LORD. *Even to the tenth generation, none of them may enter the assembly of the* LORD *forever, because they did not meet you with bread and with water on the way, when you came out of Egypt, and because they hired against you Balaam the son of Beor from Pethor of Mesopotamia, to curse you. But the* LORD *your God would not listen to Balaam; instead the* LORD *your God turned the curse into a blessing for you, because the* LORD *your God loved you. You shall not seek their peace or their prosperity all your days forever.*

As if that weren't enough warning, in Psalm 60:8 God says *Moab is my washbasin; upon Edom I cast my shoe; over Philistia I shout in triumph.* Moab was where God washed the dirt off His hands. Would God want Elimelech and his family to seek the prosperity of Moab? Would God want them moving from the place of bread, even in dire circumstances, to a place where the enemies of God and despisers of His people dwelled? No. What would He want them to do? Repent of their sins and return to him with all their heart while exerting all their influence on their brethren to do the same.

Both in Deuteronomy 4 and 30 God explicitly urges His people to renew their trust, love, and obedience toward Him in the time of cursing, and He promises to relent and bring blessing in response. Over and over again they proved his mercy in the wilderness and the promised land. Their history since leaving Egypt amounted to a frustrating cycle of disobedience, destruction, repentance, and deliverance. Elimelech should have known the heart of God and cried out like Jeremiah. *Let us test and examine our ways, and return to the LORD! Let us lift up our hearts and hands to God in heaven.*[6] He should have led his family with the hope of Hosea. *Come, let us return to the LORD; for he has torn us, that he may heal us; he has struck us down, and he will bind us up.*[7] If he'd been committed to keeping God's commands, he would have played a part in the revival that lifted the famine ten years later, but instead he let his fears overcome his faith.

Living by sight

It was a sinful sojourn because Elimelech was living by sight and not by faith. There is no indication that this was a faith-induced sojourn. It was not a faith move, but a decision made solely on the basis of what they could see around them. When God led Abram into Canaan, it was a faith move, made in response to God's leadership. When God led the children of Israel by Joshua into Canaan, it was a faith move, made in response to God's direction. This move had nothing to do with faith. It was made solely on the basis of sight and circumstances. We must remember Romans 14:23. *For whatever does not proceed from faith is sin.* Even when we have decisions to make that are not clearly addressed in the word of God, those decisions should be made while seeking the Lord, trusting the Lord, and bringing all of the appropriate biblical principles into the picture as we make the decision. Anything else is sin.

It is sin when we don't believe and respond to what God clearly says in His word. It is sin when we don't consider and seek the will of God in our decisions…when we don't pray…when we don't look to God's word…when we don't seek godly counsel…when we don't wait when it is appropriate to wait for God's direction. It is not faith living. It is sight and circumstance living, and it is natural and sinful.

May God help us to trust in Him with all our hearts and lean not on our own understanding, but to acknowledge Him in all our ways. When we do that, we can know that He will direct our paths.[8] When tough choices confront us, may we offer up sincere prayer saying "Lord, I know from Your word that my life belongs to You and that my ambition in everything is to be

---

[6] Lamentations 4:30
[7] Hosea 6:1
[88] Proverbs 3:5-6

pleasing to You, and that I'm not to do one thing that violates any principle of Your Word. So with those boundaries for my life, I trust You by Your providence to give me guidance."

Majoring on the physical

It was a sinful sojourn because they majored on the physical instead of the spiritual. There was nothing wrong with Elimelech's desire to provide for his family. That is scriptural and admirable. But not even the desire to put food in our own mouths or in the mouths of our children should be our first concern. Our first concern should always be, "What is the will of God?" We should know that when we walk in the will of God, His provision will be there. Psalm 37:25 says, *I have been young, and now am old, yet I have not seen the righteous forsaken or his children begging for bread.* Our Lord gives the reason for this phenomenon in Matthew 6:33 when He says, *But seek first the kingdom of God and his righteousness, and all these things will be added to you.* Elimelech allowed his desire for physical sustenance and security to outweigh his desire for God's will to be done. The results would be nothing short of tragic for his family.

Giving reason to blaspheme

It was a sinful sojourn because he gave reason for the enemies of God to blaspheme. In verse six, Naomi acknowledges that it was God who sent the famine and then relieved it (1:6). They knew that God was intricately involved in the activities in their homeland. Leaving Bethlehem represented an abandonment of the true God's protection in favor of another's. "God isn't providing for us here, so we will go over to a place where our God isn't acknowledged, where a false god is given credit, and we will share in the provision that they enjoy."

The chief deity in Moab was Chemosh. Chemosh was very much like Baal of the Canaanites. He was thought to be the god of fertility. He was thought to be the god who controls the forces of nature. He was thought to be the provider of bread. So here is a family who claims to worship the God of heaven, departing from the land where God placed them and sojourning to a land that seems to be filled with plenty, but where all of the glory is being given to a false god. This move would have been viewed as an admission of the superiority of Chemosh. Can you imagine how the news spread throughout Moab and how they scoffed at Yahweh when this Jewish family sought shelter beneath the wings of Chemosh?

This leads to some very simple but important questions that every Christian ought to ask before making any decision. Will this honor or dishonor God? Will this give the enemies of God an opportunity to be confirmed in their unbelief? Will this say to them that He is not real and cannot be counted on to provide for his people? Will it be a practical acknowledgment that their ways are better than His ways? If the answer is yes, then we are in danger of committing the same sin as Elimelech, a sin so serious that when David gave reason for God's enemies to blaspheme, the Lord had to take away his son in order to mitigate its effects. (2Sa 12:14)

Running into temptation

It was a sinful sojourn because it placed his sons in a position of great temptation. Elimelech probably didn't plan on staying in Moab for 10 years, but when you begin to take steps down the wrong pathway, you never know how far it will take you. As it turned out, his two boys ended up marrying foreign wives, contrary to the specific instruction of God. Deuteronomy 7:1-4 says:

> When the LORD your God brings you into the land that you are entering to take possession of it, and clears away many nations before you, the Hittites, the Girgashites, the Amorites, the Canaanites, the Perizzites, the Hivites, and the Jebusites, seven nations more numerous and mightier than you, and when the LORD your God gives them over to you, and you defeat them, then you must devote them to complete destruction. You shall make no covenant with them and show no mercy to them. You shall not intermarry with them, giving your daughters to their sons or taking their daughters for your sons, for they would turn away your sons from following me, to serve other gods. Then the anger of the LORD would be kindled against you, and he would destroy you quickly.

It is true that Moab wasn't on that list, but that is only because the idea that some of God's people would leave the land of their inheritance to live among their enemies would have been unthinkable at the time the Law was given. Clearly, the principle of avoiding intermarriage with those who don't worship the true God would have applied to this case as well. By disregarding this principle and raising his sons in the midst of foreigners and idol worshippers, he placed them in a position of great temptation to disobey God in their marriage relationships. They stumbled under the weight of their father's ungodly choices.

Do the decisions that you have been making lately place you in a position of unnecessary temptation? God doesn't take us out of the world; He makes us holy in the midst of it, but there is a difference between the temptations that arise as we live our lives in a sinful world, and jeopardizing ourselves and our families by purposely moving outside of God's revealed will. Matthew Henry put it well. "Those that bring young people into bad acquaintance and take them out of the way of public ordinances, though they may think them well-principled, and armed against temptation, know not what will be the end thereof." The frightening thing about this kind of sinful choice, is that by the time you acknowledge it, it may be too late, which is why exposure to temptation must be taken into account <u>before</u> we make each decision.

The Sadness (1:3-5)

Notice the result of this sinful sojourn:

- Death – Elimelech is the first to go, and is followed by his two sons. This is not surprising since their names mean "sickly" and "pining."

- Disobedience – Before their demise, the sons took Moabite wives. The fact that God used one of them in the line of the Messiah does not clear their guilt, but it does magnify God's grace.

- Destitution – Not only was Naomi devoid of male protection in the midst of a patriarchal society, she was far from her home and far from her God, viewing her agony as the effect of His antagonism. From man's perspective Naomi's condition was beyond desperate. It was hopeless.

What Naomi doesn't know is that in the midst of this heartache and darkness the providence of God is at work. Despite the disobedience of this family, God is going to use them tremendously, to bring His good purposes to pass.

It is true that our gracious God often finds a way to bring good out of our sinful decisions, but that does not excuse us from learning the lesson of Elimelech. If you say you are one of God's people, if you say that "my God is king" (the meaning of Elimelech's name), then shouldn't you desire and trust His will above everything else? Whatever you're facing right now, whatever may have you afraid, whatever may have you thinking about leaving, do you believe he will protect and provide for you right there in the midst of it? What if you've already departed? You've run to the place of compromise and ease. You already made the choice that Elimelech made, and you're seeing the inevitable death and destitution that come as a result. Are you ready to return? Will you acknowledge that you've walked out of the way? Will you acknowledge that you've compromised the truth? Will you acknowledge that you've disobeyed the Lord? Will you allow the Lord to show His grace and mercy mighty in your life? Will you allow Him to meet you where you are in the land of Moab and do something in your heart that only He can do? Is that what you want? If so, you need only ask. Genuinely, earnestly, confidently ask Him.

There's a time when leaving leads to loss, and that's when leaving means walking outside the will of God, to do what seems best in your own eyes. Thank God, there is also a time when He leads us home.

13

2
WHEN GOD LEADS US HOME
(1:6-7)

Sometimes you cannot move forward until you are willing to go back. Sometimes God must take us back to the place of our disobedience, the place where we departed from His way, before we can progress on the right path. In fact, there are times when our lives almost become cyclical. We keep coming back to the same issues and tests, and until we learn to respond obediently in those situations there is a sense in which we don't progress. We see an example of that here in the book of Ruth.

Ruth 1:1-5 revealed how Elimelech's family disobeyed God. They took a sinful sojourn from Bethlehem to Moab. Three widows are the proof of how dearly their decision cost them. They left Bethlehem a full family in the midst of famine and now in Moab there are three graves and three destitute women. Their desperate situation confronted them with an all-important question. "Where do we go from here?" In verses 6-22 God supplies the answer by taking Naomi back to the place of her family's disobedience so that she could experience His joy and blessing in her future. It's true, on the surface it appears that she makes this decision all by herself, but we know from the rest of this book that God's providential hand was at work in her decisions.

The Choice to Return (1:6-7)

In the midst of the darkest time of her life, Naomi makes a life-altering decision. Hearing that the famine is over in Israel, she abandons her dwelling place of the last decade and returns home along with her daughters-in-law. Although this was the right decision, it was also a despondent decision for the following three reasons.

She was hearing but not experiencing.

God was now blessing the place where Elimelech's family had once lived, but because of their sinful sojourn, Naomi isn't there to experience it. There is loneliness and emptiness when we wander from God's place for us. When we make the choice to depart from the will of God, we make the choice to enter a spiritual desert. We enter a place where we see or hear of God working in the lives of others, but we don't get to experience any of it. That is a lonely and empty place. People around us tell of the many wonderful things that they are learning from God's Word, but we have nothing good to report. They tell of the richness and happiness of their walk with God, but we can't join in their joy because God seems far from us. They tell of the burden that they have for ministry, the zeal for lost souls, the love for God's people, but we can't relate, we can only remember what it once felt like to be in the place of God's blessing. We have known what it is to experience the work of God in us and through us, but now we only know that our hearts are cold and hard. Because of our disobedience, we are now only watching and hearing. We aren't experiencing.

The saddest thing about being in such a place is that it is entirely avoidable if we would only believe that God has ordained that our walk with Him will not always be easy. The Lord is going to take us through times of difficulty that we might learn what it is to remain steadfast and faithful and fully submitted to Him—no matter what. Our growth and maturity in Christ sometimes demand a difficult life.

She was reacting but not responding.

There is no indication in the text that Naomi has experienced any brokenness in her heart over the sin that she and her husband committed. She has a firm belief that God is against her (vs.13), but we don't see her respond to that belief as we would hope for her to: with repentance and supplication. This was not a faith move, nor did it have any spiritual motivation behind it. Her trust was not in the Provider but in the news that there was provision back home. She is still reacting to her circumstances instead of seeking the face and guidance of God.

People are still doing this. They are searching for blessing instead of setting their hearts on the one who blesses. They are like storm chasers, except they are good-circumstance chasers. What they miss is that God Himself is the greatest blessing, and their hearts can only be satisfied in Him. Because they aren't looking to Him, but are running around looking for satisfaction in their circumstances, they find that satisfaction constantly eludes them. They don't understand that there is something far worse than having leanness in your circumstances: having leanness in your soul.

This is where Naomi is. We will see it in more detail in the next section, but notice her spiritual condition here. She still has a knowledge of God and an awareness of His work around her, but her focus is skewed. She lacks the spiritual clarity and depth of perception that should be present in one of God's people. What's worse, there is no evidence of any warmth toward God, or submission to His will. She knows about God, but she isn't knowing God. That is where even a genuine believer can wander in their walk with God when they are adrift in sin and needing to come home.

She was about to lose half the family she had left

Even a large family experiences heartache at the loss of single member, but Naomi's decision would cost her one of the two she could still call kin. It was not death that would bereave her of Orpah, but decisions that would be made by the three women on the way home.

The Choices on the Return Home (1:8-18)
The choice of Naomi

Somewhere on the way back to Bethlehem, Naomi makes a choice. She decides that it isn't right for her daughters-in-law to go back home with her, and she tries to convince them to go back to their homes in Moab. Why would Naomi do this? Why would she encourage these two women to go back to a heathen land and thus to the worship of false gods? After all, verse 15 shows that Naomi was fully aware of the spiritual ramifications of the course that she was urging them to take.

She may have had pure motives. From verse 8 we know that she recognized the faithfulness these women had shown her. From verse 9 we see that she had a concern for their safety. The word " rest" is a Hebrew word which means "safe shelter." It was used technically to speak of a husband's house, a woman's safe resort. In the culture of the day, unmarried women and young widows were in great danger of servitude, neglect or licentious living. In verses 11-13, Naomi communicates that a decision to accompany her would be a decision to remain single for life. In her mind, her childlessness excluded the possibility of levirate marriage, and the Israelite young men were otherwise forbidden to marry them. Naomi hates the thought that Ruth and Orpah would never be able to marry and have children.

Sadly, she may also have had impure motives. Some wonder if this was an attempt on Naomi's part to cover her sin. If she went back to Bethlehem with two Moabite daughters-in-law, it would have been undeniably clear that her family's disobedience to God went beyond a move to Moab. It would be clear for everyone to see that her two sons married foreign women.

We don't know what was in Naomi's heart and mind, but we do know this: *she had a poor spiritual mindset.* She was still entirely focused on physical factors (marriage, children, security…), and she was still wholly void of proper spiritual concerns (the worship of false gods vs. continuing with the true

God). If you understand salvation and you know there's only one true God in this universe, and you are walking with that God, and you want your daughters-in-law to belong to that one true God, then you would never send them back to a place where they would be returning to false gods. Yet Naomi shows no concern about that. In such a poor spiritual condition, we cannot rule out the thought that Naomi had mixed motives for her choice to urge them to depart.

The choice of Orpah

Naomi's choice to send them away presented Orpah and Ruth with a choice of their own. Would they listen to the voice of Naomi and return to their people and the gods of their past? Or will they make the journey to Judah? We learn from verses 14-15 that Orpah made the wrong choice: she elected to throw in her lot with her former family in Moab. Although this decision was probably made on the basis of the practical, material concerns that Naomi raised, it included a return to idolatry, which made it nothing less than full-fledged apostasy. From every indication, these girls had adopted the worship of Yahweh when they married into this Jewish family. So, here was a woman who had been exposed to the truth about the one true God and had made an outward break from her false worship and from her heathen heritage. She even had a kind of love for the people of God, for she wept with Naomi and departed with a kiss. But she had never made a genuine faith commitment to God himself, and she had never released her false gods in her heart, for if she had, then she wouldn't have returned to them.

This is a decision that people are still making today. There are those all around us who are lingering upon the threshold of salvation. They have been exposed to the working of the true God around them. They may even have made a profession of faith in that God, but they have never truly entered into a relationship with Him. They have outwardly identified themselves with the true God, but they have never inwardly been delivered from their false gods. The evidence of this is an eventual departure from the truth and a return to whatever false god they worshipped before. They may try to make an amiable break with God's people, but their kiss is too much like the kiss of Judas.

The choice of Ruth

"And Orpah kissed her mother-in-law, but Ruth clung to her." With these simple yet powerful words the author differentiates between the mere affection of Orpah and the resolution of Ruth. Ruth decided that she was going to remain faithful to the true God. She was going to make her way to Bethlehem. This was a *spiritual decision* on Ruth's part.

Listen to her confession in verse 16. *Do not urge me to leave you or to return from following you. For where you go I will go, and where you lodge I will lodge. Your people shall be my people, and your God my God.* Now hear Boaz's understanding of her faith in 2:12. *The LORD repay you for what you have done, and a full reward be given you by the LORD, the God of Israel, under whose wings you have come to take refuge!* Both her own declaration and the testimony of those around bear witness to Ruth's genuine faith in God. In fact, because Ruth's decision here was not just about Naomi but about the Lord, it paints us a picture of what it looks like for any believer to follow Him. Notice the following six things about her choice.

1) *This was a choice motivated by love.* In verse 16a we find that Ruth's heart was set on Naomi. She was going to remain faithful to her mother-in-law no matter what. Then in verse 14 we see Ruth weeping and clinging to Naomi. This was a decision that involved both great passion and great devotion. She loved this woman. This was a love choice.

2) *This was a choice that involved a great commitment.* Based on verses 11 and 12 we know that Ruth was making this decision with the full understanding that it would probably mean a lifetime of destitution. She would have no husband, no children, no home to call her own. She would be in a place where she might be despised and rejected. This was a decision that came at great cost and commitment and yet her words to Naomi do not indicate even a hint of hesitation.

3) *This was a choice of complete identification.* She completely identified herself with Naomi's life and circumstances. Wherever Naomi went, whatever she faced, whatever associations were hers, these would be those of Ruth. What a testimony Ruth was to the love that God produces in the hearts of His people!

4) *This was a decision of complete separation.* She was making the decision to leave her family, her land, her former worship, and her former devotions. She was leaving everything that she was familiar with and all that she might have had and experienced, and all that she had ever known and found security in.

5) *This was a choice of great hope.* There is no other basis for a decision like this one. She was making this move because her hope and trust was in God. What truth about God was she hoping in? Verse 17 indicates she seems to see this commitment as a responsibility before God, so her hope is in the truth that God watches over those who walk in obedience to Him.

6) *This was a decision of permanence.* She made a lifetime decision. She wasn't giving this a try. She wasn't making a rash choice without thought. She was binding herself to God and His people for life.

Are not these qualities that defined Ruth's decision to follow Naomi the same qualities that attend every genuine decision to follow God? Are they not the essential components of the decision to trust in Christ for salvation? Is it not a decision of love? Of great commitment? Of complete identification? Of complete separation? Of great hope? And of permanence? And there is another way that the decision to follow Naomi is analogous to the decision to follow Jesus. In both cases, the choice is made in response to a divine drawing and a divine plan. We know Ruth's choice was a part of his plan, because He was bringing the grandmother of King David into her appointed place in the bloodline of the Messiah. And we know that her choice was the result of his drawing because of the otherwise insurmountable obstacles that had to be overcome. Her past was against her, for Moab was all she had ever known. Her future prospects were against her, for in Israel there seemed to be no hope. Her mother-in-law was against her, urging and persuading her to go home. The example of Orpah was against her, so to remain was to remain alone. To be frank, there was no earthly reason for her to decide as she did. But God had a plan, and in accordance with His plan she made the right choice.

The Changes Evident on the Return Home (1:19-22)

God was sovereignly acting in and through these three real-life choices. When the dust settled, there was one worldly woman walking away from Israel and there were two redeemed women walking toward it. Both were brokenhearted, but one, Ruth the Moabitess, was hopeful. The other returned to Bethlehem noticeably changed. The losses Naomi sustained during her sojourn had altered her appearance to the point that she was almost unrecognizable. The women of the town ask in apparent disbelief "is this Naomi?" and her answer explains the changes that had transformed her visage.

Naomi returned a bitter woman

"She said to them, 'Do not call me Naomi; call me Mara, for the Almighty has dealt very bitterly with me.'" Naomi left Bethlehem with the name pleasant. When she and her family abandoned God's clearly revealed will, they forfeited the sweetness of obedience. The result is that she comes back calling herself bitter.

Naomi returned a broken woman

Her explanation continues with "I went out full, but the Lord has brought me back empty. Why do you call me Naomi, since the Lord has witnessed against me and the Almighty has afflicted me?" She left the place of God's will whole. She returned home broken. She experienced the truth of Psalm 39:11 *When you discipline a man with rebukes for sin, you consume like a moth what is dear to him.*

Naomi returned a blessed woman

Blinded by her bitterness and brokenness, she couldn't see that she also returned a blessed woman. Verse 22 tells us what Naomi failed to mention during her lament to the women of the town: *So Naomi returned, and with her Ruth the Moabitess, her daughter-in-law, who returned from the land of Moab. And they came to Bethlehem at the beginning of barley harvest.* She couldn't see it, but she was blessed. In his sovereign goodness God led this woman back to the place of her departure. Yes, she lost her husband. Yes, she lost her sons. But she still had her life, and God had given her another opportunity to do what is right in His sight, and a daughter-in-law who was as faithfully devoted to Him and to her as humanly possible. She couldn't see the smiling face behind the frowning circumstance. She couldn't see the rays of light piercing through the darkened clouds. She was blessed, but all she could see was her affliction.

George H. Morrison once wrote, "Nine-tenths of our unhappiness is selfishness and is an insult in the face of God." We can't see our blessings because we're so focused on ourselves. We can't see how merciful God has been to us, how kind and how patient. This is where Naomi's heart was at the close of chapter one, but the urgent question now is, where is your heart?

Is your heart in a place like Orpah's was? Are you someone who has come to the threshold of salvation? Have you been exposed to the true God and outwardly identified with Him without ever really knowing Him? If so, I exhort you with all my heart not to walk away from the true and living God. Recognize where you'll be spending eternity and repent and place your faith in the true and living God, knowing the only way to be reconciled to Him is through the death of His Son Jesus Christ. I urge you to turn to Christ and to put your faith in Him.

Or perhaps your heart is in a place like that of Naomi. Maybe you know the true God, but you're out of step with Him. You've walked outside of His will, and the effects are evident in your life. You went out full, but you've coming back empty and broken. You went out pleasant, but right now you're bitter. You know Him to be the true God. You attribute what's going on around you to Him, but there's not been any brokenness or sorrow over your sin, and as a result there has not been any real repentance. You've been satisfied to keep on walking outside of what you know is God's will. Would you repent with a broken heart? Would you turn to the Lord and plead with him, crying out "Dear Father, would You restore unto me the joy of Your salvation?"

Or is your heart in the place of Ruth's heart? By God's grace and mercy, you've been saved and are now stepping forward and pursuing the Lord. If that's you, you've made the right choice! The Lord saved us that we might live for Him with all our hearts, all the time, all the days of our life. And may we evidence a love that says, "Where You want me to go is where I want to go. Where you want me to be is where I want to be, and those people who are known by Your name, they're my people, and you're my God."

May we live for Him like that, and may He teach us to love His people in such a way that we are willing to be identified with them even in their difficult circumstances, even when it's hard to love them, even when it costs us to love them. May we love them with the same love with which our God has loved us.

3
THE PROVIDENCE OF GOD
(2:1-3)

The book of Ruth teaches us about the providence of God in a dramatic way. It reminds us that God has not distanced Himself from His creation. God did not create the universe simply to step away and let it run itself. He is involved at every moment, not only preserving the work of His hands, but also directing it toward His eternal purposes. We are reminded of this truth here in chapter 2. It focuses our attention on God's good providence.

What is meant by the providence of God? Stated simply, God's providence is His sovereign control over what He has created. To be more specific, it is "the continuous activity of God whereby He makes all the events of the physical, spiritual, mental and moral realms work out His purpose. This purpose is nothing short of His original design for creation."[9] God is so big, so wise and so powerful that his control includes everything from the orbit of each celestial body to the motives, thoughts, words and actions of each human being. And there is absolutely nothing which can thwart His perfect purposes: not sin, not Satan, not even the decisions of mankind.

This divine quality permeates the book of Ruth. It is especially impressive here in chapter 2; for on this day when Ruth, Naomi, Boaz, and his workers are making decisions, God is quietly executing his grand design. We see his plan unfolding first in the brief profile of Boaz in verse 1, and second in His place of provision for Ruth and Naomi in verses 2 and 3.

A Profile of Boaz (2:1)
The Holy Spirit is introducing Boaz to us at this point so that we will look forward to and have a better understanding of the divine appointment

---

[9] Modified very slightly from Thiessen, Henry Clarence, *Lectures in Theology*, revised by Vernon D. Doerksen (Grand Rapids: Wm. B. Eerdmans, 1979), p. 123

that Ruth and Boaz will have later on this day. Ruth knows nothing about him as she begins this day, and apparently Naomi has not been thinking about him either, because she seems surprised when Ruth relates her conversation with him (17-20). Their meeting was not the result of a search or a human agenda; it was the result of sovereign guidance. In order for us to grasp the significance of this coming encounter, the writer fills us in on a few facts about the man Boaz.

A kinsman of Elimelech

The family connection of Boaz to Elimelech may seem to be a superfluous detail, but it is an essential part of the Lord's plan. The original readers of the book of Ruth would have immediately perceived that this minute revelation contained the potential to change the lives of Ruth and Naomi forever, but most modern readers won't give it a second thought. Why this discrepancy? Why should the fate of these women rest on this Boaz-Elimelech relationship? The answer is found in the Torah. Hundreds of years before the days of Ruth, God gave specific laws concerning kinsmen and their responsibilities, laws that were potentially life-changing for the Jews, but easily overlooked by us. A kinsman had three basic duties which are listed below alongside references for further study.

1) If poverty had compelled his brother to go into slavery or to dispose of his land, then a kinsman was to redeem (buy back) his brother and his brother's inheritance according to his ability. He would also do this on behalf of his brother's family in the event of his brother's death. Leviticus 25:23-28

2) He was to avenge any fatal violence against his brother. Numbers 35:10-29

3) If his brother died without leaving a son, he was to raise up a successor to his brother by marrying his brother's widow. Deuteronomy 25:5-10

What if a redeemer refused to do what the law required? If he avoided the fate of Onan (Genesis 38:10), he would still face the following: *And if the man does not wish to take his brother's wife ... then his brother's wife shall go up to him in the presence of the elders and pull his sandal off his foot and spit in his face. And she shall answer and say, 'So shall it be done to the man who does not build up his brother's house.' And the name of his house shall be called in Israel, 'The house of him who had his sandal pulled off.'* [10]

---

[10] Deuteronomy 25:7-10

What if there was more than one potential kinsman redeemer? Once again, God's directions were clear. The nearest of kin bore the responsibility, but if he was unwilling or unable to discharge his duty the next in line would take his place. We will soon see these God-given rules working to carry out His plan for the future of Boaz, Ruth, the whole kingdom of Israel, and the rest of world.

A man of means

By mentioning his influence or wealth (depending on the translation), the Spirit of God is already letting us know that this potential redeemer has the capability to solve all of Ruth and Naomi's financial issues instantly.

A Place of Provision for Ruth (2:2-3)

Ruth's circumstances

Unlike Boaz, Ruth and Naomi were not blessed with abundant resources. In fact, they had nothing. But whether they knew it or not, their place of poverty was exactly where God wanted them to be. He intended for them to have nothing in order that He might use their barrenness to channel them toward unimaginable blessing.

When Ruth announces her intention to go into the fields of grain and glean, she is referring to a means of providing for the poor that was set forth in God's law wherein an owner could send a team of reapers through his field only a single time. This allowed the poor to come behind them and gather what was left. Some say that as much as 30 percent of the crop would be left in the field after the first pass. Taking the wheat from the field to the oven was a difficult process for female gleaners like Ruth. It involved cutting and carrying the stalks and then threshing what was harvested to separate and eliminate the chaff, all before grinding the wheat into flour. It was hard manual labor, but it was a way that poor people could live and eat.

Leaving these leftovers in the field wasn't optional for the landowner. If he wanted to abide in God's blessing then he had to obey God's repeated command (Lev 19:9, 23:22, Deut 24:19). Just as God established the law of a kinsman redeemer for the protection of the truly vulnerable, so He set forth laws of gleaning for the same purpose. And although the main point of this passage has nothing to do with finances, there are some powerful principles to be gleaned from this law that we dare not leave behind.

- It reminds us about ownership. Even though someone owned a piece of property, God still had every right to tell them what to do with it. So God is the actual owner of everything we possess; we are simply stewards of His things. When we refuse to give what God calls us to give, we are living in practical denial of this truth. We may be acknowledging God's ownership with our lips, but we are declaring our own independent authority with our lives.

- It reminds us of the need to be generous. God promised His blessing to the field owner with an open hand toward the poor. We will see later in the chapter that Boaz met and exceeded the minimum requirement of the law by inviting Ruth to eat with him, promising her his protection, and instructing his workers to drop some of the stalks that they had harvested on purpose so that she could come along and pick them up easily. Is it any wonder that God exceeded a minimal blessing in return by making Boaz both a type and an ancestor of the Christ?

- It reminds us of God's concern for the poor and needy. Is it possible that we have seen so much abuse of generosity that we have become calloused to the cries of the lowly? May the Law remind us that despite all the abuse of His generosity that God has seen, His heart has not become calloused. He has a great concern for those who are poor and in need, for the widow and the orphan and the stranger. That is why He put this law in place.

- It reminds us of how the poor are to be helped. God has the best plan for how to help the poor. He doesn't give them handouts; He gives them opportunity. He allowed them an opportunity to benefit from the blessings of others, but to get those blessings they had to go out and work for it. Remember, this was a judicial law that reflected a moral principle. It's a principal repeated in the New Testament (2 The 3:10), and one that we can and should continue to apply today in the way that we help the poor.

As we consider the circumstances of our two widows in light of this law, we understand that if Ruth resorted to gleaning, then she and Naomi had no other means to survive. They were at a point where the only chance to eat and live was through finding someone with the godliness and generosity to allow Ruth to glean in his field. Even once she found such a patron, Ruth would have to go out in the hot sun, cut stalks of grain all day, and then go through the arduous process of threshing those stalks in the evening. She was committing herself to tiring and humbling labor in order to provide for Naomi and herself.

Ruth's character

Through these difficult circumstances we learn very valuable things about Ruth's character. The following qualities show us who she really was.

- She was gracious. She is about to engage in painstaking labor for her mother-in-law, and her attitude is still one of gracious respect. She isn't haughty. She isn't bitter. She isn't regretting her decision to identify herself with Naomi. She is respectful, aware of authority, and gracious in her demeanor. This is one of the greatest marks of godliness. When someone is respectful of authority, gracious in their service, and kind to all in the midst of a stressful situation, it says that they have a real and genuine submission to God. Only God can give this kind of insight and produce this kind of character.

  What kind of attitude do you offer your service with? Young people, what is your attitude when your parents call upon you to do something? When is the last time you asked if you could serve them? Christian worker, what is your attitude when it comes to the job that you do for the people who are in authority over you? Christian servant, what is your attitude about the service you give around the church, and what is your attitude toward those who are over you in the Lord? Don't miss out on the chance to represent Christ well through your service. Godly character is revealed in a gracious spirit, and that was the spirit of Ruth.

- She was giving. This woman was unselfish and sacrificial in her willingness to give. She didn't desire to go into the field for her herself alone. She was as concerned about Naomi's needs as she was about her own. Even when Boaz was kind enough to allow Ruth to sit down and eat with him and his reapers, Ruth couldn't fill her stomach without thinking of Naomi (vs.14 & 18). This is exactly the kind of heart that Christ produces in His people. Not a heart that says "me," but a heart that says "us," and a heart that says "others" (Philippians 2:3).

- She was godly, and here we can see her godliness in several respects. We see it in her faith, for what she was doing was no safe thing (vs.21-23). We see it in her industry, for she was willing to work hard in order to fulfill her responsibilities. We see it in her faithfulness, for she could easily have changed her mind and returned to Moab. We see it in her humility, for this was not a prestigious position, and she did not set herself about it with an attitude of entitlement but of gratitude for the opportunity to work for a living.

- She was guided. Was this an accident or was this divine providence? Was it an accident when Elimelech's sin led his family into the country of Moab where this young woman lived? Was it an accident when she married the young man Mahlon? Was it an accident when

Mahlon died, leaving her a widow and free to marry another? Was it an accident when God visited his people and gave them food, thus drawing Ruth and Naomi back to Bethlehem? Was it an accident when she decided on this particular day to go and glean in the fields and came to the field of one named Boaz? Did Boaz just happen to be a kinsman? Did he just happen to visit his field at the same time she was there? Did a Moabitess just happen to stumble into the lineage of the Messiah? No, this was the sovereign hand of God bringing His eternal plan to its appointed place. This was providence. This is the same providence through which God still controls all the events of this world. There is not one molecule running loose in the universe, or in your body for that matter. There is not one unforeseen problem in your life, nor are there any that you are unprepared for in Christ.

Do you know the God who created you? Are you trusting Him and His plan for your life? Are you godly and gracious and giving like Ruth? The kind of circumstances you find yourself in is not what's important. What matters is the kind of character you allow the Lord to produce in your life.

4
A DIVINE APPOINTMENT
(2:4-16)

Like many other portions of Old Testament narrative, the book of Ruth represents both real history and rich typology. It is an authentic account of a family, and a woman, and a man. More importantly, it is the record of how God worked in and through all of their lives to accomplish His purpose. Yet within this straightforward story the Holy Spirit has embedded additional spiritual truth through the art of typology. Every worthy anecdote contains elements of foreshadowing, and the book of Ruth is no exception. Its historical characters are used by God to illustrate future realities of immense importance. So as we study Boaz, Ruth, and their relationship with one another we will learn of the relationship that Jesus Christ, our Kinsman-Redeemer, has with the Church, His bride. And what we will learn through this comparison is that underlined redemption is a work of love.

Redemption is not a cold, heartless act carried out by a redeemer void of passion. No, a real redeemer acts because his heart is set on the object needing redemption. When Boaz redeemed Ruth, it was because he loved her, and when the Lord Jesus redeemed His church, it was because He loved us (Eph 5:25). And just as Ruth's encounter with Boaz was a divine appointment, so you and I become aware of God's love and respond to that love according to His sovereign timetable through the convicting, drawing ministry of the Holy Spirit of God who brought us face to face with Jesus. So the beginning of a great romance is before us in this initial encounter of our two protagonists, and it breaks down naturally into three parts. Boaz inquires about Ruth, involves himself with her, and intercedes for her.

Boaz Inquires About Ruth (2:4-7)

In verses 1-3, Ruth makes a decision to go out and glean on behalf of herself and Naomi. She is hoping to find a field where she will be allowed to follow the reapers and, through hard labor, bring home something to eat. On this same day Boaz just "happens" to visit this field of his to see how things are going. Now let's finally see what ensues.

His greeting

Right away we are told something about Boaz that wasn't revealed to us in verse 1. We know he is a man of means and a relative of Elimelech, but until now we've known nothing of his spiritual condition. If verse 4 reveals nothing else it certainly shows that Boaz is a man of faith. He was a man who not only had a relationship with the Lord, but who carried that relationship with him wherever he went. When he comes to the field to check on his workers, it isn't with a proud or intimidating attitude, but with the joy and graciousness of God, saying *the Lord be with you* And he's met with *the Lord bless you* in return. The owner is praying for the blessing of God upon his workers, and the workers are praying for the prosperity of God upon their boss! This is how it should be with godly people. Believers can't compartmentalize their lives. They mustn't have one compartment for Christian activities and another for life as a businessman or an employee. Your attitude at work, regardless of your position, should reflect your relationship with the Lord. Apart from Him, this kind of kindness is impossible, but Christ not only gives his followers the ability to imitate Boaz, He gives them the responsibility (Mat 5:16). In Christ, we can. In Christ, we must. And in Christ we will, so long as we remember this crucial principle: We do not bless others because they bless us; we bless others because God has blessed us. In order to be successful witnesses in our workplaces we mustn't wait for our boss, coworkers, or employees to treat us fairly. Instead we take the initiative in doing good, and we persevere in well-doing regardless of whether they ever reciprocate it.

His question

Not long after he greets his workers, his attention is arrested by a new face in his field. So Boaz asks the manager of his reapers a question that would change his life forever, *Whose young woman is this?*

The response

The manager of the reapers fills Boaz in on what had happened that morning. He explains who she is, how she came to Bethlehem, how she entreated them to gain access to his field, and how she toiled all day for her food. This manager was obviously impressed by Ruth, and now Boaz was aware of her worth as well.

Our conclusion

What we have in verses 4-7 is a divine appointment. God has brought

Ruth to the field, He has brought Boaz to the field, and He has put them in contact with each other by stirring up interest in Boaz' heart.

If Ruth chooses another field, this meeting doesn't happen.

If Boaz doesn't visit this field on this day, it doesn't happen.

If Boaz visits the field while she is resting,

If she doesn't catch his eye,

If he has something else on his mind,

If for any other reason he fails to inquire about her… it doesn't happen.

God has arranged this appointment before the foundation of the world. There is no power in existence that could have prevented it.

Dear friend, think about your life. Think about the divine appointments that you have unknowingly kept. Think about how you met your wife or your husband. Think about the pathway that your life has taken, how you came to have the children that you have and the job that you have. I hope that you see the hand of God in every appointment of your life, because only then will you see that for every appointment He has a purpose.

Gary, a member of our church, told me about his young son's divine appointment with some poison ivy. About a week after he recovered from his rash he was out playing baseball with his dad when one of the balls rolled to where the open field met a wooded lot. In the midst of chasing the ball, the boy suddenly stopped and turned saying "Dad, why don't you go get it? There may be poison ivy over there." So Gary set off to retrieve the ball until he too stopped in his tracks, only this time it wasn't the fear of poison ivy that froze him, but the fear of a poisonous snake—a copperhead lay coiled a couple of feet from the ball.

So when that child was scratching those bumps and feeling quite miserable a week or two before, an almighty, all-knowing, all-loving God already knew of a snake sitting beside a baseball, and was using his misery to prevent a catastrophe. God's providence works not only in circumstances, but in our thoughts, motives, intentions, and even our fears in order to bring about His unsearchable will. What kind of wisdom is required to weave such seemingly unrelated events together, and to do so for billions of humans, animals, and angels simultaneously such that nothing in all the universe goes amiss?

But as impressive as God's daily providence is, there is something more astounding by far, and that is the way His providence interacts with His saving purposes. Think about your salvation. Think about how you came to hear the gospel. Think about how you came to really understand who Jesus is, for the first time. Think about the person who shared with you and the circumstances surrounding that moment. Think about all that could have prevented you from faith, and acknowledge that the time of your salvation was a divine visitation. Before He made a single atom, He made an appointment with you. He took it upon himself to ensure that you would keep it.; then He met you there and called your name in order to redeem you.

Boaz Involves Himself with Ruth (2:8-14)

The image of Ruth has caught the eye of Boaz, and the story of Ruth has caught his heart; now he makes the choice to involve himself in her life. As we see this budding relationship, we cannot help but see a picture of God's grace toward us. Remember that Ruth has gone out looking for favor on this day. She is poor. She is destitute, and she is on the lowest rung of the social ladder. She really deserves nothing. She has no claim on anyone. Her only hope is unmerited favor. Her only hope is grace. What a picture of how lost sinners come to find Jesus Christ! There are six aspects of the grace of God toward helpless man that are visible in the kindness that Boaz pours out on Ruth.

1) *Boaz takes the initiative.* Remember that Ruth has nothing. There is no reason why the owner of a field, a wealthy man of reputation, would show any special interest in her. She has no right to expect it, nor does she expect it. As far as she knows, the owner of the field will see her as one more poor gleaner. She does not try to befriend him in any way. Yet Boaz takes a special interest in her, and he is the one to initiate a relationship with her. This is exactly what happens when God saves a sinner by His grace. Every person is born into this world in a state of spiritual destitution. We were

Dead in our sins (Eph 2:1).

Without spiritual resources or recourse (Rom 5:6).

Estranged from and rebellious toward God (Col 1:21).

Yet God took the initiative in that He sent His Son into the world to die for sinners, and He took the initiative in that He chose us, and sought us, and drew us to Himself (1Jo 4:19, Joh 15:16). God took the initiative in establishing our relationship in every way—in the plan of salvation, in the provision for salvation, in the pursuit of the sinner, and in the production of saving faith in the heart. The implications of this truth are life-changing. If Jesus really paid it <u>all</u>, then <u>all</u> to him we owe.

2) *Boaz speaks to Ruth.* For a wealthy landowner to speak to a poor, female foreigner was unusual, if not unthinkable, hence her response of humility and wonder (10). If Boaz doesn't speak to Ruth, there was no way she would speak to him. When God saves a sinner, something far more amazing and wonderful takes place. God actually speaks to that person through His Word. There is a call issued, and it is an effectual call, for it always leads to salvation (Jud 1:1, Rom 1:5, 2The 2:14, Rom, 8:30).

3) *Boaz promises to protect Ruth and to provide for her.* He says, "my daughter" for a couple of reasons. First, he was older than she was (3:10). Second, she was going to be treated like a member of the family, much like the way that God treats those He calls. Not only does He take foreigners and treat them like His children, He officially makes them His children by adoption. And just as Boaz promises to protect Ruth from harm, so our Redeemer shields those who take refuge in Him. He brings them into a place of protection where they are eternally safe from the consequences of their spiritual poverty (1 The 5:9, Joh 10:28). Boaz provides for her by quenching her thirst and later satisfying her hunger. Our Lord does the same for us. He is the living water and the bread of life. He promises to meet our every need in every realm of life.

4) *Boaz' grace is overwhelming to Ruth.* She can hardly believe that he would take notice of her. She humbles herself before him, admitting her place of helplessness. She judges herself unworthy of his attention. When we understand what God has done for us in salvation, we will fall on our faces as well. God does not have to save us. He is under no obligation to initiate a relationship with us. So when He does, humble amazement is the only appropriate response. "Who am I that you would take notice of me? Who am I that the Sovereign God would speak to my heart and show me the way of salvation through His Son?"

5) *Boaz knows of Ruth before she knows of him.* Ruth knows nothing of Boaz as she first forages in his field, but Boaz knows of her. He has already heard of her faith. He already knows of her kindness and her godliness. His motives for this kindness toward her are pure; he wants to be a channel of grace through which God can pour out His blessings upon this young woman. This is actually where the comparison breaks down. It is true that God knew of us before we ever knew of Him, but far from that knowledge motivating Him to save us, it would have moved Him to destroy us were it not for His great mercy. He knew that we were wicked. He knew that there was nothing good in us. He knew that there was nothing in us that would have invited His redemption. He knew that we did not love Him, nor would we seek Him (Rom 3:10-11, 5:10). There was something virtuous and attractive about Ruth that Boaz was aware of, but there was nothing virtuous or attractive about us, and God knew that very well.

6) *Boaz' grace is received by Ruth.* She accepts his favor, she acknowledges his kindness, and she admits her unworthiness. To put it simply, she trusts him and receives his help, offering nothing but gratitude in exchange. This is exactly what happens in salvation. We simply believe God. We accept His favor, we acknowledge His kindness, and we admit our unworthiness. We receive his help with nothing in our hands and gratitude in our hearts.

7) *Boaz fully satisfies Ruth.* He shares with her from his riches as he becomes for her like a servant. So we share with Christ in his riches, because he became for us like a servant. We share in the riches of His mercy, love, and grace (Eph 2:4-7). We share in the riches of His wisdom and knowledge (Rom 11:33). We share in the riches of His glory (Phi 4:19). We share in unfathomable riches (Eph 3:8).

Boaz Intervenes on Behalf of Ruth (2:15-16)

We have overheard Boaz inquire about Ruth to his manager, and we have listened in and drawn out truths from his involvement with her. Now we see him intervene on her behalf. What exactly does he do for her? First, he gives her a new position by officially granting her the right to gather from his field. She is no longer subject to the whims of the manager; she is permanently permitted on the premises. Next, he gives her a new provision by commanding his men to purposely pull out grain from their bundles to facilitate the work of gleaning. Lastly, he gives her a new protection by ordering his men not to insult or rebuke her. She has come under the care of the owner of the field. Yes, for the first time since her husband died, she has someone strong watching over her. Even if Boaz never saw Ruth again, the security, supply, and safety that he has afforded her would have tremendously blessed both her and her mother-in-law as long as they lived, as they now had a nearly unlimited supply of what they needed to survive. But of course that is not how the story ends.

Before moving on to see this relationship blossom, each of us must ask himself, "Have I ever come under the care and provision of the Lord of the Harvest? Have I come to know the Kinsman-Redeemer, the Lord Jesus Christ, who gives to His people a new position and a new provision and a new protection? Do I know the one who is intervening and interceding for His people when they're not even aware of it? And if so, am I still amazed by Him? Do I still fall to the ground in recognition that my salvation was not because of me but in spite of me? That it was result of pure and passionate love?" Oh, how thankful should the Redeemer's bride be!

5
LIVING IN HOPE
(2:17-23)

There are very few attitudes that affect the human experience as profoundly as hope. When a person has biblical hope, they have joy. They have an inner assurance. They have a positive outlook on life. But when hope is absent, despair is inevitably present. There's a sense of emptiness that defies alleviation. There's a somberness that grips their life and alters their perception of every situation.

From the perspective of the Word of God, we understand that only a Christian can have genuine hope. The world has no answers, no stability, no sure knowledge about this life or the future, and therefore no hope. But once a person comes to know Christ, not only do they have a hope, they have a *sure* hope. It's not a shallow "hope so" feeling based on overly-optimistic fantasies, but the internal assurance of the fulfillment of God's promises. It's a confidence that we will not face the future without His help. It's the knowledge that He has already provided for everything we will ever need in Christ. Such a hope was Paul's prayer for believers in Romans 15:13—"*may the God of hope fill you with all joy and peace in believing, so that by the power of the Holy Spirit you may abound in hope.*" And such a hope is God's plan for His people in every place and time.

As we continue to look at the life of Ruth, we'll see some encouraging truths about living in hope. This young foreigner has found grace in the fields of Boaz and returns home to Naomi with a new spring in her step because she has a new hope in her heart. Her example reminds us who have found the grace of God that we have every reason to live in hope until the day of redemption. Why should our countenances be downcast and depressed and somber and fearful and fretting? Should not our faces reflect a heart that's hopeful and joyful and positive and assured and confident until the day when all we know by faith becomes sight and all that God has promised is brought to completion? May God use the model of His humble servant Ruth to invigorate us with hope and to instill in us this joy. Our exploration of this passage will follow the three movements of the text, beginning with the end of Ruth's fateful day in Boaz' field.

Ruth's Return Home (2:17-18)

Remember that something wonderful has just happened to Ruth in this barley field. Boaz, the kinsman of Elimelech and owner of this field, has initiated a relationship with her. He has shown her unmerited favor and has blessed her in an unexpected way. After this encounter she heads back into the field until evening to complete her task, but you can imagine just how different her work was now. When she began that fateful morning, she didn't even know whether she would find a field to labor in. Now she's been blessed beyond imagination. When she did find the right field, she was just another gleaner, but now she knows the owner, and he has personally assigned her a new position, a new provision and a new protection. And all these blessings are not just hers for the day, but for the whole length of the harvest.

Ruth labors in Hope

After such a turnaround, can anyone doubt that she has a happy and hopeful heart? Boaz bestowed food when she was hungry, water when she was thirsty, and rest when she was weary. Her favorable circumstances resulted in aching arms as she returned home with 30-40 pounds of barley: enough to feed her little family for two weeks! Not bad for one day's work! So even though her job did not change from morning to evening, we can be sure that her attitude did. Her heart had been set at rest. She had a sure knowledge about her immediate future, and she had a new relationship that she could rejoice in. The same things are true for everyone who enters into a relationship with the Redeemer of souls.

The field doesn't change when we come to know God's grace in Christ, but our relationship to the owner of the field does. In light of our new position, we now work the same field in a very different way. God doesn't take us out of the world, and He doesn't relieve our human responsibilities in it. Instead, He makes us different in the midst of it and makes us see it in an entirely new light. Now we know that the owner has taken special notice of us, and not only that, has promised to provide for all of our needs, both physical and spiritual. He is the bread that fully satisfies and the water that forever quenches. He offers repose for weary souls so that we labor with a heart relieved of worry and laden with joy. He banishes fear by ensuring our eternal protection. Everything before us and everything inside us changes when we enter into fellowship with the Owner of this world.

Child of God, rejoice that you're not living your life in the dark, apart from Him and His providence and promises. You know that there's One at work in your life right now, conforming you to the image of His Son. You know the promises that He has given you for the present and those that concern your future. You know He's guiding you and preserving you unto a sure and good destination so that even though you're living in the same world that you lived in before you were a Christian, you now view it with a whole new perspective. Everything is different.

An old hymn, "This is My Father's World," celebrates this very thing. It starts,

This is my Father's world, and to my listening ears
all nature sings and round me rings the music of the spheres.

This is my Father's world, I rest me in the thought
of rocks and trees of skies and seas — His hand the wonders wrought.

A Christian is one who understands that everything is explained by God, and therefore a Christian is one who is able to see Him and glorify him in all realms of life. A Christian sees the handiwork of God in the sky, sea, rocks, and trees, and proudly proclaims 'this is my Father's world!' For a Christian, every day is the day that the Lord has made, and not one thing comes our way but what has first passed by the Father's permission. No matter how dark things may seem and how far this world has strayed from what is true and right, He is *still* in complete control.

This is my Father's world, O let me ne'er forget
that though the wrong seems oft so strong God is the Ruler yet.

This is my Father's world, the battle is not done,
Jesus who died shall be satisfied and earth and heav'n be one.

We can rejoice in our Father's wise control. Do you ever get discouraged by sin? Do you ever look around at this world we live in and wonder "Can it go any farther? Can it get any worse?" What a comfort in that moment to know that our God is on His throne, and He's not seated apathetically, but reigning actively. And He's willing and able to use all things, even evil, for His glory and the good of His beloved people.

Are you now laboring in hope? Can others see the light of your bright future shining in your eyes? Are you hopeful or despairing? God is not glorified by joyless servants. God is not glorified when we act like it's miserable to know Him and miserable to serve Him. God is glorified when your hope is written on your face. You serve a generous God. Are you living a jubilant life?

Ruth is doing the same work in the same field, but the atmosphere of her heart has been transformed and her countenance transfigured, for she knows she is in the merciful arms of the owner.

Ruth returns full

When she finally returns home (2:18), what a difference this day has made! She went out empty, and she comes in full. She went out helpless, and she comes in hopeful. She went out without direction, but she comes in with a good report. And she is now going to share with her mother-in-law out of the overflow of Boaz' blessing. Do you remember the day when you went out one kind of person and came in another? Do you remember the day when you met the Lord of the harvest? Do you remember the day when you went out empty but came in full, went out helpless but came in hopeful? Do you remember the day when you went out in the morning without any meaningful direction, but returned in the evening with a good report? If so, then are you being faithful to share with others out of the overflow of the gracious blessing that your Redeemer has shared with you?

There's no doubt that what happened to Ruth that day was amazing and worthy of sharing with anyone who was willing to listen, but does it compare to what happened in your case? You go out one morning and you're dead in your trespasses and sins. You do not know your Creator. You go out one morning and you are enslaved to your sin, to the world's system, and to Satan. You go out one morning and you are under the condemnation and wrath of a holy God. But you come in that evening having trusted Jesus as Lord and Savior, and now you're suddenly alive and free and accepted. You have been made a child of the living God. I wonder, are you ready to tell someone about that? How can you have something so unbelievable happen to you without ever desiring to tell anyone? Such a thought is not only improbable. It is impossible. So, if there is no desire to share of the overflow of Christ's blessing, could it be that something unbelievable hasn't happened in your life? Could it be that you don't have a burden to witness because you don't know the thrill of being radically transformed from the inside out, or the miracle of having your eternal future flipped on its head? Or is it the case that though you once marveled over being made an object of grace, you now hardly take notice of it? This chilling, hardening, and shrinking of the heart is an astounding thing, but it really does happen, even to pastors and teachers. May the eagerness of this widow to open her mouth and share with Naomi drive the indifference from our hearts.

Ruth's Report and Naomi's Response (2:19-21)

How will Naomi respond to Ruth's report? Earlier we saw that Naomi described herself as a bitter woman (1:20-21). When Ruth asked permission to go work in the field on this day, the only recorded response was, "*Go, my daughter."* No words of encouragement or promises of prayer are offered. As far as we know, this is the same hurting woman who returned home empty from Moab. Soon we'll see whether Ruth's news can uplift her spirit, but first notice these two unmistakable characteristics of hope.

1. Hope is visible. Naomi knew that someone had shown extraordinary kindness to Ruth before she spoke a word. She wore hope upon her face and she carried hope in her arms, 30-40 pounds of it! Ruth's work would never have yielded so much unless someone had shown her special attention and generosity. May we each live our life in such a way that God's overflowing generosity will be manifest before and beyond our verbal testimony. May God's attention toward us, and His affection for us, be so evident that the lost must inquire into the reason for the hope that is in us.

2. Hope is humble. Don't miss how Ruth's humility subtly affects her report of her encounter with Boaz. Do you notice that there is no mention of the commendation that she received from his lips? Her account withholds the fact that Boaz was moved to help her by Ruth's good testimony and faithful care for her mother-in-law. Ruth takes the time to report the kind deed of Boaz, but she apparently doesn't care to recount his kind words about her. Christian hope ought to produce even greater humility in us because, unlike Ruth, we did nothing to arrest God's attention and garner his grace. This is why the doctrine of election, when rightly understood, will never puff up God's people. On the contrary, it deflates pride. It creates a keenness to give credit to Him who deserves it.

Now that Naomi has noticed Ruth's transformation and heard her humble explanation, she offers up a hopeful response.

Naomi has hope because of who Boaz is

She rejoices because Ruth has received sympathy from a near relative. Suddenly there is the prospect of their being redeemed out of poverty, and even the potential for him to redeem Ruth out of widowhood and raise up a son to carry on her family name (hence the mention of God's remembrance of the dead). God has not forgotten his foolish servant Elimelech, even though he deserved to have his name forsaken on account of his sinful sojourn. It's impossible to overstate how life-altering this information is for Naomi, and thus it is impossible to recreate her joy. It marks a paradigm shift in her thinking about the future. She thought she was without hope and without God in the world, but now she knows that she could not have been more wrong.

Naomi has hope because of what Boaz did and said

Not only did Boaz' identity give Naomi hope, so did his provision for them. As we've already seen, he wasn't content to help Ruth for just a day. He promised to provide for her throughout the harvest, so this ephah of barley is only a first-fruits of all that Boaz has guaranteed. His kind deeds and words mean blessing, security and hope for their future.

Naomi has hope because of the kindness of God

Before this, she viewed the hand of God as constantly chastening. Now she sees that same hand as graciously giving. The Hebrew word from verse 20 translated "kindness" is the Hebrew word חֶסֶד (chesed). It refers to God's gracious, loyal love. God's "chesed" never did forsake Naomi or her family. Despair had blinded her to it, but now hope has opened her eyes.

I want you to see that even though Naomi recognizes the kindness of God, she also recognizes that it is stationed in this one person Boaz. And I want to submit to you that in the hope of these two women we have a picture of the Christian's hope. Our hope in God is stationed in a person.

- 1 Timothy 1:1 *Paul, an apostle of Christ Jesus by command of God our Savior and of Christ* **Jesus our hope**

- 1 Thessalonians 1:3 *Remembering before our God and Father your work of faith and labor of love and steadfastness of* **hope in our Lord Jesus Christ.**

As was the case with Boaz, our hope in Him is because of who He is, as well as what He has done and said. He is the one who became like us in order that He could legitimately be our kinsman and thus our redeemer. His cross-work, resurrection, and intercession give us security in the present, and his innumerable promises impart hope for our future. Do you realize that no matter how you feel or what you are going through, you can rejoice in hope if you set your focus on Jesus Christ? Jesus is the reason for our hope. He is the anchor of our hope. He is the focus of our hope. If you are a believer and if you have lost the joy of your hope, it can only be because you have lost your focus. You have forgotten the source, security, and sustenance of your hope. Refocus your attention on the Lord Jesus. Set your eyes on the Author and Finisher of your faith. Run the race with your eyes fixed on Him (Heb 12:1-2). Labor with gladness, knowing who He is and what He has done and what He has said.

Ruth Remains in Hope of Redemption (2:22-23)
The counsel of Naomi

The suddenly hopeful Naomi counsels Ruth to heed the instructions of Boaz by not being found in anyone else's field. Ruth's protection depends on it. Ruth's prospect of redemption depends on it. And Ruth's reputation as a grateful and loyal woman depends on it. How shameful it would be for her to abandon the one who has shown such attention to her! But as sound as it was, Naomi's advice was hardly necessary. Why would Ruth want to leave the field of such a gracious and generous owner? Why would she want to go anywhere else?

Can't the same thing be said of us and our Redeemer? May we purpose in our hearts to stay in the field of the one who showed us favor and showered us with blessings. I mean the field of His will for us. I mean the field of His truth. I mean the place where God has promised to keep us safe. When you consider how kind He's been to us, how good He's been to us, how gracious, how perfect, how truthful, how merciful, why would we ever want to insult Him by wandering outside His field? The place of obedience is the only safe and proper place for the believer. Why would we ever want to go anywhere else?

Have you departed from the field of the One who has shown you such grace? Have you, with an ungrateful heart, decided that the fields that had left you empty before you ever knew Him might somehow fulfill you now? Have you forgotten how empty and how devastating and how destructive sin is? If so, I know it has cost you the joy of your salvation. Don't sacrifice real joy at the altar of guilty pleasure a moment longer. Don't barter your soul's assurance for cheap thrills. It's time to repent and to return to the One who has been so kind to you and to live for Him with all your heart.

The continuance of Ruth

How does Ruth respond to Naomi's counsel? Just as her character and common sense would suggest: she listens! But just because this was the right choice and the obvious choice doesn't mean it was an easy choice. The barley harvest was March and April. The wheat harvest was June and July. So for four months (five counting the month of May when work was slow) she toils steadily on in hope of her future redemption.

What a picture of Christians as we labor in His field! Whereas Ruth's redemption still seemed uncertain to her, Christ has already redeemed us from our spiritual poverty. He's promised us a future inheritance beyond imagination to be received at the end of the harvest. What does he expect of us in the meantime? To toil on. To serve Him with steadfastness month after month in the hope of our final and complete redemption, the redemption of our bodies. He expects us to keep working in our waiting.

6
A REQUEST FOR MARRIAGE
(3:1-18)

When chapter three begins, the harvest season is coming to a close. Ruth's work in the field of Boaz is ending, and the time has come to test his willingness to fulfill the duty of a kinsman. Naomi desires marriage for Ruth, and she is going to give her daughter-in-law guidance toward that end.

The previous chapters leave us with no doubt that God is putting this marriage together, but it is instructive that He uses human choices to do so. This is one of many of examples of the glorious way that God works *through* human desires and decisions. So we will continue to learn about God's providence in chapter three, but we'll see more than that. By considering the choices of Naomi, Ruth, and Boaz we also have the opportunity to examine the choices that lie before us, especially decisions related to marriage. What you have in this chapter is a woman requesting marriage in accordance with the law of God, the provision of God, and the customs of her culture. Such a request reveals lessons for all those seeking marriage as well as those who parent them. These lessons will surface as we make our way through the four divisions of the text: Naomi's plan, Ruth's presentation, Boaz's response, and Ruth's return.

Naomi's Plan (3:1-4)
Naomi's sense of responsibility

The first thing that strikes us about Naomi's plan is that she feels responsible to help her daughter-in-law enter into marriage. When Naomi says *"my daughter, should I not seek rest for you, that it may be well with you?"* what she has in mind is marriage. In fact, this is the same language Naomi used to refer to the security of marriage. 1:9 *"The LORD grant that you may find rest, each of you in the house of her husband!"* What thoughts might be motivating Naomi's words in 3:1?

- She cares for Ruth's future security. As already mentioned in previous chapters, for a single woman to live in this culture and in this land at this time was not a safe situation To be in a husband's home was to be in a place of shelter.

- She cares for Ruth's future happiness. The word used in the phrase *"that it may be well with you"* has to do with gladness or pleasantness. In effect, Naomi is saying "daughter, I want you to be happy. I want you to be glad. I want you to rediscover the joy of marriage."

- She knows of God's law concerning the kinsman redeemer, and counted on Boaz' obedience to it. Her love and responsibility for Ruth combined with her awareness of God's righteous rules are what inspired Naomi to create her impactful plan.

Naomi's strategy to have Ruth wed

Not only does Naomi express a sense of responsibility, she also articulates a strategy.

- She reminds Ruth of her relationship to Boaz in 2a.

- She informs Ruth of the activities of Boaz in 2b. Ruth needed no explanation for this phrase, but most of us do. After the harvest came the process of winnowing. There would be a place, usually on a high hill, where they would toss the threshed grain and husks up into the air. The husks would be blown away, and the precious grain would be left to be gathered into bags. The process would often go on long into the night accompanied by celebration and thanksgiving to our Lord the provider. If the grain remained on the threshing floor overnight then the owner and workers would sleep beside it to avoid being robbed.

- She instructs Ruth concerning preparation in 3a. Evidently a bath was in order after a long season of reaping. Talk about timeless counsel! If you want to catch a husband, or a wife for that matter, it's a good thing to be clean. But cleanliness isn't the only thing that never goes out of style, neither does soft, fragrant skin. Hence the instruction for Ruth to anoint herself with what would likely have been aromatic oils. Finally, Naomi knows what a difference it makes to see a coworker wearing something other than her work clothes, so she encourages Ruth to put on something nice.

- She instructs Ruth concerning her presentation in 3b-4, including the timing of it. She isn't to rush in while he's working, eating, or drinking, but to make sure everything else on his mind is finished. She also tells Ruth the place where she's to present herself: at his feet while he is lying down to sleep. And she instructs Ruth as to the manner in which to present herself: not by speaking, but by silently lying and waiting on him to speak.

This is bold advice to be sure, but we must be careful to distinguish between boldness and impropriety. Nothing Naomi suggests would have violated either biblical law or the decorum of the day. Arranged marriages were the norm in the ancient Near East, and Deuteronomy 25 gave women the right to initiate the redemption process. Out of concern for Ruth's future, Naomi acts as if she were Ruth's biological mother. She devises a plan that is daring, but in no way indecent. But how does it apply to us?

What responsibility do we have as parents when it comes to the matter of the marriage of our children? Consider the following five principles taken from throughout the Word of God.

1. We should model the kind of marriage God wants for our children. One of the sad things I see in the church is that parents want something for their children that they are not willing to work for themselves. They underestimate the tendency for children to live out in their marriages whatever they saw lived out at home.

2. We should believe, live, and teach the biblical convictions that make for a godly home. Convictions like the permanence of marriage, the importance of worship, and the existence of distinct roles for man and wife, ought to be read from the Bible and reinforced through our lives.

3. We should teach them how to discern between right and wrong, including what to look out for and what to look for in a spouse. We need look no further than the book of Proverbs for a biblical example of this aspect of parenting.

4. We should pray for their future spouse and teach them to do the same. It's never too early to begin this process and never too late until their vows are exchanged.

5. We should give them practical guidance in how to go about establishing a godly relationship. As much as we might wish otherwise, the fact is we don't live in the days of arranged marriages. But that does not revoke our responsibility to influence and advise.

Ruth's Presentation (3:5-9)

How does Ruth respond to the concern and strategy of her mother-in-law? She responds with submission and obedience. With regard to both her preparation and her presentation, she did all that was commanded, lying down at the feet of the Boaz while his heart was full of the joy of the harvest, not drunk on wine as some suggest.

Although I wouldn't recommend Ruth's approach in the world we live in today, there was nothing immoral about it. This cultural expression seems strange to us, so some read it in light of modern standards and assume that more went on upon the threshing floor than the text explicitly states, but the reaction of Boaz demonstrates that he understood her gesture perfectly. Ruth was not asking to share the covers for one night, she was asking for the covering of marriage for life. It's an offer Boaz gladly accepts because she is a worthy woman, that is, a woman of virtue. This commendation is yet another confirmation of Ruth's godly intentions. Worthy women are not employed in the art of seduction.

That said, Ruth didn't show up in a burlap sack! There's no doubt that the world places too much emphasis on appearance, but sometimes the church reacts by ignoring it altogether. We should teach our children that inward beauty is foremost, but that appearance does have some importance. Obsession with it can indicate vanity, but neglect of it can indicate laziness. What we want to indicate is that we are neat, and orderly, and godly, but not so "spiritual" as to ignore the body altogether. The Bible doesn't teach us to neglect the body on behalf of the soul, but to take care of the whole person, so we must encourage both boys and girls to present a good testimony in the way that they care for themselves. Otherwise, don't be surprised when they have a hard time finding a respectable date! If every time a young man sees a young woman she looks unkempt, if her hair is messed up, if she looks like she's ready to wrestle him, then she shouldn't be surprised if he never shows interest in her! She may truly love the Lord, but if she looks like she loves wrestling, he will likely never get to know her. This may seem silly, but it's a practical matter that is worth consideration.

Ruth heeded her mother-in-law's advice with regard to more than just her appearance. She followed all of Naomi's instructions with precision and without hesitation. Young people still do well to heed the guidance and the instruction of their parents. Naomi's heart was with Ruth, and the heart of every godly parent is with their child. Young man or young woman, know that their desire is not to ruin or place constraints upon your happiness. They love you, and their desire is to guide you in a godly and safe path. Often their desire is to keep you from the heartache they once felt, but even if they aren't speaking from a position of experience, they are speaking from a position of authority as long as they are speaking according to the Word of God. Which leads to another lesson from Ruth and Naomi's interaction: we who are parents must be sure that the guidance that we give to our children is the guidance of God. It is not our job as parents to make our children happy but to teach them to be holy. It is not our job to acquiesce to what they want or to make them into what we want them to be; it is our job to guide them in the way that God wants. As our children grow our influence over them may wane, but that does not relieve us of the responsibility to warn them of evil, exhort them unto good, and give them practical advice on how to live a bright life in these black times. My adult children may disregard me, but I hope they will never be able to blame me for staying silent when I should have spoken loving words of wisdom into their lives.

Boaz' Response (3:10-15)

How would the potential redeemer respond to this unexpected encounter? In a way that shows that he was truly a godly man. The more I study this man, the more I am impressed and amazed by his character. His reaction proves that even in the dead of night the Lord was on his mind. Can you imagine waking up in the dark to find somebody at your feet? I know my first thought would probably not be to bless that person in the name of the Lord! Not only is the Lord continually before his mind, but his affectionate choice of words reflects the love and the kindness of God. He was almost certainly startled, but his address is gentle nonetheless. She has made herself vulnerable to rejection by her brave request, so he sets her heart at ease by referring to her as "my daughter." Who can say what those words of comfort and assurance meant to her at that fateful moment? Finally, he shows that he is a man who loves godly virtue, for what attracts him to Ruth's proposal is not her elegant clothes, or even her clean, soft, fragrant skin, but he is allured by her righteous life. We know this by the praise he pours out on her in 10-11.

Boaz' praise

He praises for her loyal love. The word translated "kindness" in verse 10 is the same word (*chesed*) Naomi uses for God's loyal love in 2:20. Ruth was not only the beneficiary of this kind of love from God, she was also the benefactor who showed steadfast love both to Naomi and Boaz, and he recognized, admired, and now celebrated this rare quality in Ruth.

He praises her for her purity. Evidently Boaz was quite a bit older than Ruth. She could have disdained his age and decided to look elsewhere for remarriage. She could have disregarded the law of God in Deuteronomy 25 which instructed her not to marry outside her family. She could have, but she didn't. She waited with purity and patience for her day of redemption.

He praises her for her virtue by pointing out that the whole city now knows her to be a worthy woman. I pray every young woman reading this understands that you cannot, you will not, attract to you the kind of person that you refuse to be. You may say, "I want to marry a man who loves the Lord loyally, who will love me faithfully, and who will guard the sanctity of our marriage." You say you want a man of virtue and strength that you can admire and look up to. At least I hope you say those things! But if you desire that kind of man, then you must be that kind of woman. Be a young woman of loyalty, of purity and of virtue, because like attracts like. The principle of sowing and reaping applies to finding a spouse just as much as it does to every other pursuit. Those who sow ungodliness in themselves will eventually reap it from their spouse.

Young man, are you looking for a woman who is praiseworthy in the sight of God? I know I made the case that no one should neglect their appearance, but there's a difference between believing that a godly person should be neat and orderly and well-taken-care-of and presentable, and determining that the person you agree to marry will have to be a knockout!

The Scripture says this: "*Charm is deceitful, and beauty is vain, but a woman who fears the LORD is to be praised*" (Prov. 31:30). You may marry the beautiful woman of your dreams only to end up in a miserable marriage for the rest of your life if that beauty doesn't love the Lord. Or you may marry someone who loves you for your looks only to have her leave you when she finds someone who looks better. But if you find a Ruth, then nothing, not the side-effects of cancer, not the scars of a car wreck, not the slow decay of time, will be able erode your relationship, because it will be built on the solid rock of Christ and not the shifting sand of physical attraction.

Boaz' promise

Not only does Boaz praise his future bride, he promises to do for her what she has requested. A promise from a man of integrity is enough to banish anxiety. How do we know Boaz was a man of integrity? Notice the confidence Naomi has in his word "*Wait, my daughter, until you learn how the matter turns out, for the man will not rest but will settle the matter today.*" That kind of confidence stems from a sterling reputation. If Boaz says he'll take up your case, he won't rest until the matter is settled.

Can the same be said of you? Are you a man of your word? Are your commitments as certain as guarantees? There's not a person on this earth whose conscience is not pained at the thought of some failure in this area, but is the desire of your heart and pattern of your life one of trustworthiness? If not, you can look to the one called "faithful and true" for forgiveness and transformation. He is the only hope—not only for the dishonest, but for sinners of all sorts.

Boaz' priority

So why does he worry about this other relative at all? Some might say that Boaz was trying to find a way out of marrying her, but I don't believe that for a moment. When a godly man like Boaz has a godly young woman who desires to be his wife, there's no reason to think that he will be anything other than eager to oblige. That's not the issue. The issue is that although Boaz desired Ruth as much as she desired him, he had a commitment to the word of God and to the order that God had ordained. He understood that it was not yet his right, that there was a closer relative who must first decide. In other words, he knew he would be violating the Word of God to marry her immediately, and even for a woman like Ruth, he was unwilling to do that.

Don't you know that people could have given them a myriad of reasons why they didn't need take this additional step? "Listen, Boaz, God clearly put this together. How do you explain her presence in your field? How do you explain your arrival at just the right time? How do you explain that you are a near relative of hers? Why waste time and risk losing her with this additional step? She loves you, and you love her. What stands in the way?" For Boaz, the Word of God stands in the way. He has a higher priority than love for a woman, and that's love for the Lord. That's the foundation for a great marriage. The foundation for a great marriage is not love for one another. The foundation for a great marriage is the love that both husband and wife have for God. If you don't love the Lord more than you love the person you're marrying, then you're building upon a faulty foundation. And if you would violate the Word of God to marry that person then, clearly, you don't love the Lord more than you love them. What about you, young man? Can you say that setting aside the truth of God's Word is never a viable option, even if keeping it might mean you couldn't be with the woman you desire?

Boaz' protection

Boaz tries to suppress the knowledge of Ruth's visit to the threshing floor. Why? There's only one reason. He knows that she did nothing inappropriate. She knows that she did nothing inappropriate. But if word of their meeting got it, how would the townspeople know that they did nothing inappropriate? Boaz is zealous to protect Ruth's reputation. He knows that appearances matter. Any potential spouse who isn't scrupulous to protect your reputation is either too foolish to know the importance of appearances, or too selfish to care. Are you the kind of man who abhors the thought of harming the testimony or reputation of the person you say you love?

Boaz' provision

We can't know with certainty how much barley Boaz sends Ruth home with that morning because the text doesn't supply the name of the measure that's used, but the most likely estimate is 60 pounds. This would be twice what she gleaned on her first day in the field and about as much as she could carry home. Ruth has not come there for grain, so what is the point of this gift? Boaz is making a statement. He wants her to know about his commitment to care for her should she indeed become his bride.

It's an unpopular truth, but I'm absolutely convinced that Scripture places the responsibility to provide for the material needs of the family on the shoulders of the husband alone. This is not a co-responsibility; we're just living in a day when men prefer to shirk their God-given duty. I know this idea sounds old-fashioned, and I realize that the modern standard of living is designed for two-income families, but isn't it wonderful that God delights to make a way where it seems that there is no way? Isn't it a relief that God can and does provide through unimaginable means when we commit to honor His Word? Young man who desires marriage, I ask you, are you prepared to provide for your bride?

Ruth's Return Home (3:16-18)

In these concluding verses, Naomi learns that her plans have prospered; the Lord blessed her sense of responsibility and worked through her strategy. Ruth begins a period of waiting to see what the will of the Lord, and the rest of her future, will hold. Boaz proves his worth yet again by insisting that Ruth bring grain back to her mother-in-law, suggesting that he would soon assume responsibility for Naomi as well.

We learn a lot in this chapter, don't we? A lot that challenges us, a lot that calls for obedience, a lot that calls for repentance. Whether you are a parent charged to think and act on behalf of your children, or a young person on the verge of some of life's defining decisions, the commitments this chapter calls for will both guide you and change you. May God's grace help us to take these principles to heart and apply them to our lives.

7
THE KINSMAN REDEEMER
(4:1-10)

At the end of chapter three we saw Naomi's confidence in Boaz as a man of action. Her confidence was not misplaced. When we come to the fourth chapter we immediately see Boaz taking action. At the same time, God is taking action. God is bringing to completion the story He planned from before creation and began in Ruth 1:1. He brought this young woman from Moab to Bethlehem, to the field of Boaz, to the heart of Boaz, to the threshing floor of Boaz, and now he is bringing her into the home of Boaz. Through it all, God has not only demonstrated His providential control over the lives and affairs of people by planning a marriage that would ultimately result in the Messiah being born in Bethlehem; He has also created a union that pictures a much greater relationship of redemption. In this union we see a picture of the relationship between those who have been saved by God's grace, and their kinsman redeemer, the Lord Jesus Christ. At least 15 times in this chapter the words redeem, buy or purchase appear, making redemption the clear theme of the rest of the book. Boaz the redeemer its main character.

Boaz Calls a Conference (4:1-6)

In ancient times, the gate was the entrance into the city, and it served more than one purpose. It was a meeting place for business people and townspeople. It was a courtroom where the elders of the city would meet to hear and try a case. It was a public forum where transactions took place and contracts were established. Boaz went to the gate hoping to come across the near kinsman who had the first right of redemption.

The man's urgency

Verse 1 indicates that Boaz goes directly from the threshing floor where Ruth left him to the gate of the city. He knows what he needs to do and sets out to do it speedily. There's no doubt that Boaz understands God's involvement in the situation. As we've journeyed through this book we've noted that he's lived in constant awareness of the presence of God. But his awareness never leads to inaction. He knows God is working, but he also knows that God's involvement does not diminish his own need to act, so he determines to resolve the matter straightaway.

I point out his exigency because if we're not careful to think like Boaz, we can use the sovereignty of God to excuse our sinful inactivity. We forget that God has not only ordained the end of the matter, but the means of accomplishing it as well. We can act as if our only job is to faithfully wait on Him to do it all. But the fact is that God has called us to a life of synergistic action. He is at work in us and through us, accomplishing all that He has appointed to take place. Boaz realizes this and hurries to the gate, devising a plan along the way.

The man's strategy

Let's notice the obvious. Boaz goes to best possible place. The gate of Bethlehem is not only the most likely place for him to encounter the potential redeemer, but it is also the ideal location to collect witnesses, purchase property, and make binding promises. He's using common sense! He's using normal means. When we come to believe in the sovereignty of God we don't check our brains at the door! Isn't it carnal to think that God's will can be carried out through your own plans? I don't call it carnal; I call it biblical. I call it wisdom.

The Lord's activity

The Holy Spirit inspired the author of the book of Ruth to write in a remarkable way. Those who don't acknowledge God might describe it in terms of a love story with some scattered religious remarks. But even children with an awareness of God can see His hand behind every human action in the script. Those who have a relationship with God read that Boaz "sat down there. And behold, the redeemer, of whom Boaz had spoken, came by," and they recognize that there was nothing coincidental about that moment. The terse wording is meant to communicate that God blessed Boaz' strategy by sending the right man right away. The same God who has orchestrated every note of this symphony has used their normal decision-making processes to lead this mysterious man across Boaz' path.

THE KINSMAN REDEEMER (4:1-10)

The Lord's commentary

Don't miss the fact out of all the times this man is referenced his name is never mentioned. Even in English it's apparent that the writer deliberately withholds this man's identity, but in Hebrew it's unmistakable. The word translated "friend" is a Hebrew idiom which has a similar meaning to the phrase "so and so." Turn aside, so and so! It's not that Boaz didn't know his name. It's not that Boaz didn't actually use his name at that moment. It's that the Holy Spirit of God purposely chose not to record it. There's been some debate about why his name was left out, but the probable explanation is that God didn't think his name worthy of mention because he wasn't willing to do the honorable thing. We've already seen from the book of Leviticus, that it was a big deal to refuse to redeem your relative and their property. Such selfishness was rewarded with spit in the face and verbal humiliation. "Here's the guy whose sandal has been removed; here's the shoeless man!" Or in other words, "Here's the guy who didn't do the right thing; here's the man without honor!" God's commentary upon this interaction is that Boaz' name was considered worthy of remembrance for millenniums while so-and-so's wasn't worth mentioning at all.

The man's integrity

Boaz is about to take official action. He knows there is a protocol to follow and is determined to take the appropriate steps. We know that later in history *ten* became the official number of men necessary to transact a business deal. Maybe this had already become common practice in Bethlehem. He calls the proper number of elders and then states his case honestly, without a single word that might discourage the man from becoming the redeemer. Either the unnamed man would seize this opportunity to acquire the property that Naomi's poverty forced her to sell and raise up children for the fallen, or he would pass on it, but nothing would be done under the table, even for a woman like Ruth.

How does the closest relative respond? Initially with desire: not only does he agree to purchase the property, but he seems eager to do so, for the "*I*" in Hebrew is emphatic. His answer could be translated "*I, I* will redeem it." He puts the case forward and he says, "Now, will you redeem the property?" Perhaps he views this as a great business opportunity, that is until Boaz informs him that whoever redeems the land must also redeem the widow Ruth and raise up sons to carry on the name of the deceased. At this point his desire for the deal turns into disdain, for he realizes that the offspring of his union with Ruth would be considered Mahlon's and would inherit the property upon coming of age. He has no interest in raising up a son who would not be his own. He has no interest in buying the property, only to serve as its steward until that son of Mahlon comes of age. Suddenly, the business deal doesn't seem so sweet. Suddenly, he realizes he can't afford such a purchase without jeopardizing his own inheritance. Now we see why his name wasn't worthy of remembrance!

Boaz Makes a Commitment (4:7-10)

In verses 7-8 Boaz is formally handed the relative's sandal, and thus, the right of redemption. Given this opportunity, Boaz officially purchases the property in verse nine and publicly commits to marry Ruth and raise up an heir who would perpetuate the name of the dead. And so the very thing that he longed for comes to pass. God has given him the desire of his heart. He was at work through Boaz' activity and strategy, through ordinary human means, to bring His divine agenda to completion.

What do we learn from it? Aside from the practical observations about the cooperation of God's sovereignty and human responsibility that we have already noted, there are some spiritual observations worthy of our attention. There are similarities between Boaz' role as Ruth's kinsman-redeemer and Christ's role as our Kinsman-Redeemer that are more than coincidental.

The Meaning of Redemption

The act of redeeming something or someone is literally "to set free by paying a price." Something or someone is in bondage. It is under someone else's control or it is in jeopardy, so the redeemer comes along, pays the price, and sets them or it free from whatever was threatening. That is what Boaz did for Ruth and Naomi. And that is what Jesus Christ has done for us who know Him. The Bible says that all people are born into this world in bondage to sin and to Satan and to the world's system and to their flesh.

- Ephesians 2:1-3 *And you were dead in the trespasses and sins in which you once walked, following the course of this world, following the prince of the power of the air, the spirit that is now at work in the sons of disobedience. Among whom we all once lived in the passions of our flesh, carrying out the desires of the body and the mind, and were by nature children of wrath, like the rest of mankind.*

- John 8:33-34 *They answered him, "We are offspring of Abraham and have never been enslaved to anyone. How is it that you say, 'You will become free'?" Jesus answered them, "Truly, truly, I say to you, everyone who practices sin is a slave to sin.*

It's amazing how much we hear today about liberation. Everyone, it seems, is battling for some set of rights. Whether it be women's rights, children's rights, or LGBT rights, everyone seems to be clamoring for some kind of freedom. Yet in the midst of this universal fight for freedom, have you noticed that men and women are more oppressed than ever? Not by governments or even the culture, but by their own sinful choices. Drug addiction, alcohol addiction, food addiction, sexual addiction, to name a few slave drivers, are more powerful and widespread than ever. The more the world calls for freedom, the more it gives evidence that it's in bondage.

Why is this the case? Because it doesn't understand what real freedom is. And because even if it did, it is powerless to set itself free. Only the Son of God can give freedom, and the only way to know that freedom is on the basis of the price He paid to acquire it. Sin had to be atoned for, and when you trust in the resurrected Christ and the merits of His life and death for the forgiveness of your sins, you are set free from all that truly enslaves you.

- John 8:36 *So if the Son sets you free, you will be free indeed.*

- 1 Peter 1:18-19 *knowing that you were ransomed from the futile ways inherited from your forefathers, not with perishable things such as silver or gold, but with the precious blood of Christ, like that of a lamb without blemish or spot.*

- Mark 10:45 *For even the Son of Man came not to be served but to serve, and to give his life as a ransom for many.*

- Revelation 5:9 *And they sang a new song, saying, "Worthy are you to take the scroll and to open its seals, for you were slain, and by your blood you ransomed people for God from every tribe and language and people and nation.*

The Marks of the Redeemer

Not just anyone could serve as the redeemer. This is why Naomi rejoiced to hear that Ruth had met Boaz. She knew this man was qualified to redeem them. To serve as the kinsman redeemer, one had to meet four requirements.

A blood relative

Only members of the same physical family could exercise this right. So to redeem all humans would require someone from the family of humanity. Animals don't qualify. Angels don't qualify. Even God, before taking on a sinless human nature, didn't qualify. So Jesus Christ had to become our blood relative in order to redeem us. He became a man of flesh and blood so that He could die for mankind on the cross. Hebrews 2:14 says: *Since therefore the children share in flesh and blood, he himself likewise partook of the same things, that through death he might destroy the one who has the power of death, that is, the devil, and deliver all those who through fear of death were subject to lifelong slavery.* And this same

Jesus will remain our kinsman for all eternity. He is the God-man and will forever be so.

A costly purchase

To be the kinsman redeemer, you had to be able to pay the ransom price. This is why it was important that Boaz was a man of wealth (Ruth 2:1). Do you realize that no one else could afford the cost of our redemption? No one has the means to atone for all the sins of all of those who will believe, except the Lord Jesus Christ. In fact, it wasn't possible for our redemption to be secured by money. Our redemption required the price of precious blood. Only a perfect substitutionary sacrifice would do. A sinless man would have to die for sinful men. Psalm 49:7-9 and 15 says: *truly no man can ransom another, or give to God the price of his life, for the ransom of their life is costly and can never suffice, that he should live on forever and never see the pit... But God will ransom my soul from the power of Sheol, for he will receive me.*

A willing purchase

Just because someone was a near relative of suitable means didn't guarantee that they would choose to redeem. For redemption to occur there needed to be a willingness to sacrifice one's possessions for the sake of the dead and the desperate. Boaz counted the cost, and chose to act anyway; he was willing to risk anything in order to redeem Ruth.

Dear friends, may we never forget that Jesus did not have to die for us. God would have been perfectly justified if He had left us all to perish. If salvation is in any way owed to us by God, then it ceases to be explained by grace. Will you stop reading and reflect on the fact that you had a willing Savior, a Savior made willing only by the goodness in His own heart? Ephesians 2:4 says: *But God, being rich in mercy, because of the great love with which he loved us, even when we were dead in our trespasses, made us alive together with Christ— by grace you have been saved.*

A willing groom

Finally, it counted for nothing that a redeemer was prepared to purchase the property if he wasn't willing to wed the widow! The closest relative to Naomi had the means to redeem and was willing to buy the property, but he was reluctant to marry Ruth. But because of the great love that he had for God and for Ruth, Boaz committed more than his money that day at the gate. He committed his heart. He committed his life.

We have a kinsman in Christ who didn't just take us out of sin, He joined us to Himself. He betrothed us to Himself, and one day He will formally marry His bride. Revelation 19:6-8 foretells the joy of that day: *Then I heard what seemed to be the voice of a great multitude, like the roar of many waters and like the sound of mighty peals of thunder, crying out, "Hallelujah! For the Lord our God the*

Almighty reigns. Let us rejoice and exult and give him the glory, for the marriage of the Lamb has come, and his Bride has made herself ready; it was granted her to clothe herself with fine linen, bright and pure."

Do you have the eyes to see what was happening when Jesus was arrested in the garden? When he was rushed through mock trials? When He was mocked and beaten and spat upon? When a heavy cross was laid upon His back and He carried it to Golgotha? When nails were driven into his hands and feet? When the cross was dropped into its place and the Son of God hung between heaven and earth with the weight of the transgressions of the redeemed upon His shoulders? Do you have the eyes to see that a price was being paid? Because of the great love he had for God and for us, the Kinsman Redeemer was paying the price to set His bride free.

8
THE REDEEMED BRIDE
(4:11-12)

If Ruth 4:1-10 paints a picture of our redeemer through the actions of the man Boaz, then 11-12 gives us a glimpse of His redeemed bride through the blessings pronounced on the woman Ruth. Although Ruth is not present in this scene, the words of the witnesses in response to Boaz' commitment portray the blessed relationship that Christ has with us, His Church.

The Witnesses (4:11a)
The joy of a godly relationship
The reaction of the witnesses to Boaz's commitment to Ruth is one of unadulterated joy. They are genuinely happy for this couple; they are excited about their future and rejoicing in the opportunity to be involved in it. Isn't it wonderful when the people of God are able to sincerely rejoice with a bride and groom because their relationship with each other is clearly in the will of God? I wish every marriage of professing Christians were a cause for godly people to rejoice, but too often believers have a view of marriage that is not much different from that of unbelievers. What characterizes the unbelieving world's perspectives on marriage?

- The world views marriage as a traditional institution. They think of marriage as being something that has its source in humanity and society. They see it as a purely natural invention, having nothing to do with the living God.

- The world views marriage as involving only the happy couple. Because they see it as a traditional institution, the only realm that they consider is the human realm. They think it is about the man and wife; what does God have to do with it?

- The world views marriage as an optional institution. Cohabitation before marriage or instead of marriage has become the norm. The words of one "marriage expert" sum up view. "Deciding whether to live together without ever getting married or live together to 'road-test' marriage is a very individualized choice. Taking a look at the pros and cons is helpful so that you can make the most informed decision for you."[11] And this is someone who put on "marriage workshops" for 40 years! The world gives no thought whatsoever to what God has said about the matter. They don't take a look at the Scriptures to make an informed decision. They think the pros and cons and personal preference are all that matters.

- The world often views marriage as a temporary agreement. In fact, some prenuptial agreements state this view plainly. They have no confidence that it will last a lifetime. In fact, many don't even intend it to.

- The world views marriage as something to hedge your bet with. Because they see it as a temporary agreement, they think you should take legal action to ensure that you are not financially impaired when it goes south. Even after marriage, they would advise you to keep separate bank accounts just to be safe.

- The world views marriage as the expression of emotional love. It's what you do to prove that you really "love" a person. If you have powerful feelings about them, marry them! After all, the rest is just details. The fact that they are entering a lifelong covenant on the basis of fickle emotions is an afterthought.

It is nothing short of tragic to think that any Christian would be influenced by these satanic ideas, but any experienced pastor will tell you that many are. So what should a believer's perspective of marriage be?

- A Christian should have biblical standards for who they will marry. Before marriage, even before dating or courtship, there should be firmly established principles in your mind about who you will and will not pursue a relationship with. In fact, you might say that

---

[11] https://www.thespruce.com/cohabitation-facts-and-statistics-2302236 accessed September 2, 2017

there's only one kind of person that a believer should ever consider marrying. What kind? Well, another Christian of course! Could there be anything more natural than spending your earthly life with someone you will spend eternity with? Could there be anything more unnatural than choosing to live with someone who, by refusing to trust Him, despises the one you love more than anything or anyone? 2 Corinthians 6:14-16 makes this clear: *do not be unequally yoked with unbelievers. For what partnership has righteousness with lawlessness? Or what fellowship has light with darkness? What accord has Christ with Belial? Or what portion does a believer share with an unbeliever? What agreement has the temple of God with idols? For we are the temple of the living God.*

One last word of wisdom on this subject. If you truly want to marry in the Lord, then you do not want to marry someone whose relationship to the Lord is questionable. You want to marry a believer whose life is bearing fruit, someone with a track record of loving Jesus and walking faithfully (not perfectly) with Him.

- A Christian should believe that God has a plan for their marriage, and that as long as they are seeking His will, He will carry it out. Just as God meant for Boaz and Ruth to be together, I believe that God has someone prepared for every Christian who is called marry. God will lead you to a person who will perfectly compliment you, the person that He knows you need. Of course, that doesn't mean that a married person can get out of their marriage because they think they made a mistake. The moment you were married your spouse became God's best for you and that union is to be preserved. It also doesn't mean that you should wait for God to whisper your future spouse's name in your ear or write it in the clouds. No, we have already seen that God's providence works through ordinary means. What this does mean is that you should never rush into a marriage that you have misgivings about out of fear that you will spend your life alone. What it does mean is that a you should pray for God's guidance regarding the person that you should marry and then refuse to be anxious about it. If you can trust Him with your eternal future, then you can trust Him with your temporal future as well! He will lead you in His timing as you walk faithfully with Him.

- A Christian should be sobered by the lifelong nature of marriage. When Jesus affirmed the permanence of marriage in Matthew 19:8-10 to His disciples, they weren't just sobered, they were shocked! God, not man, invented, initiated, and instituted marriage to be one man leading one woman in a one flesh relationship *for life*. And He is involved in every marriage by personally joining man and wife together. That means every divorce is an assault on God's intentions and an attack on his handiwork. What does all this mean for a Christian preparing for marriage? It means that you and your future spouse should decide beforehand that divorce is *not an option* because defiance to God is *not an option*.

If you choose the wrong major in college, you can change it. If you choose the wrong job, you can change it. If you have a bad relationship with a friend, you can always change the level of involvement you have with that person. If you make a bad choice in the person you marry, there's nothing you can do to change it! Unbelievers believe this kind of sobriety will rob you of joy, but what they can't see is that a wise selection of your spouse will lead to a lifetime of joy, while it is exactly the lack of sober thinking about marriage that has brought them so much heartache.

The public nature of true love

When you really love someone, you are not ashamed of them. When you really love someone, you don't care who knows it. When you really love someone, you are ready and willing to be publicly identified with them. Boaz was public in his love for Ruth. It wasn't just the ten elders who would have witnessed this commitment; it was any townsperson whose business brought them to the gate. If someone is being married in the will of God, I would encourage them do it before the church and before their friends. I would discourage them from running off somewhere to get married in a private ceremony. Get married in a setting where you can tell everyone who is willing to listen, "I love this person, and I vow to go on loving them the rest of my life." And I would encourage married people not to let that stop after the marriage ceremony. Be public in your love for the person God gave you, not through uncomfortable display of public affections, but through words of affirmation that let everyone know how proud you are of the person you call "husband" or "wife."

The public nature of redemption

Long before Ruth ever approached Boaz on the threshing floor, he probably made plans to redeem her. In his thoughts, he counted the cost. He determined who he needed to approach and where to approach them. And then, when it was just the two of them talking on the threshing floor, they privately arranged to make their marriage a reality. But when the time came for the actual transaction to occur, there was nothing private about it. It occurred for all of Bethlehem to see and hear.

In eternity past, in the private counsels of the Triune God, our redemption was planned. But then the day arrived for the transaction to officially take place. So our Lord handed himself over to be held up to public scorn and shame, and the very cross that served as His place of sacrifice was also the platform from which He publicly proclaimed His love for us.

- Romans 5:8 *but God shows his love for us in that while we were still sinners, Christ died for us.*

- Ephesians 5:25 *Husbands, love your wives, as Christ loved the church and gave himself up for her,*

If our redeemer paid for our sins publicly and thus proclaimed His love for us publicly, then how can we be ashamed of Him? How can we insist on being private about our relationship with Him?

Their Wishes (4:11b)

After these people witnessed Boaz's commitment to Ruth, they made their wishes for this new couple known through an eloquent blessing.

Wishes for a powerful influence

Leah and Rachel were the wives of the patriarch Jacob. They bore him eight sons who founded the leading tribes of Israel. The first part of the witnesses' prayer is that Ruth would not only be fruitful, but also that through her children she would leave a legacy. "May God give your children similar honor and influence to those of the women who founded our nation."

Wishes for an honorable life and an honorable reputation

The name Ephrathah is another name for their hometown Bethlehem, and their prayer is that Boaz and Ruth would do mighty things there to further earn the respect of their community. These are true friends, are they not? These witnesses want the best for them. There's not a hint of jealousy in this crowd. That is what true love between brothers and sisters looks like. When we can honestly say that we want the blessings of God upon each other's lives, when we want each other to be prosperous and influential and even famous in our service to Christ, that is love. Have you ever prayed for a newly formed couple to act so worthily and work so excellently as to become famous for their labor in the Lord? Paul praised God that the Thessalonians had done that very thing. 1 Thessalonians 1:7-9: *you became an example to all the believers in Macedonia and in Achaia. For not only has the word of the Lord sounded forth from you in Macedonia and Achaia, but your faith in God has gone forth everywhere, so that we need not say anything. For they themselves report concerning us the kind of reception we had among you, and how you turned to God from idols to serve the living and true God.*

Their Words (4:12)
Regarding offspring
They believed that God would give Ruth and Boaz a son. Why? Sometimes God allows his purposes to become so clear through our circumstances that you feel like you can see exactly what's coming! God had undeniably brought this couple together for the express purpose of redeeming the family of His foolish servant Elimelech, and the birth of a son was the only aspect of that plan yet to be fulfilled.

Regarding Ruth
Do you recall how Ruth is referred to throughout this section? In verse five she was "Ruth the Moabitess," but in verse ten Boaz promises to make the Moabitess his wife, and from that point she is known as a foreigner no more. Now her identity is stationed in Boaz; she is the woman who is entering his house.

Do you remember Ruth's standing in society throughout this book? With the exception of Naomi, she was alone and unloved. She was a poverty-stricken charity case gleaning for her life in others' fields without a clue as to how she would survive the harvest-less winter. No longer. Now she is loved. Now she is co-owner of all the fields of Boaz. Now she is rich. Now she can rest. Now she hasn't a worry in the world, and it's all because she is entering Boaz' house.

Related Text—Our Redeemed Life—Ephesians 5:22-23
Do you remember what your life was like before you met Christ? Do you ever stop and take inventory of how much has changed in your life since you've come to know Him as your Lord and Savior? Ephesians 5:22-33 reminds us that our experience is strikingly similar to Ruth's.

We are subject to Christ
22-24 *Wives, submit to your own husbands, as to the Lord. For the husband is the head of the wife even as Christ is the head of the church, his body, and is himself its Savior. Now as the church submits to Christ, so also wives should submit in everything to their husbands.* Before, we had no one to lead us, but now we are subject to Christ, and that's a good thing! We were born with rebellious hearts toward God, but by the regenerating power of the Holy Spirit and by virtue of the new nature, we've been forgiven! We are now willingly subject, joyfully subject, to the Lord of glory.

We are loved by Christ

25 *Husbands, love your wives, as Christ loved the church and gave himself up for her.* Jesus proved God's love for us publicly. We know now that we are never on our own. Our destiny is joined to Christ's because of His loyal love for us. I thank God for the fact that a husband and a wife are joined together by God, and share the same destiny for as long as they live. One of the most wonderful things about being married is that you don't have to go through life alone. When there's heartache, you go through it together. When there's rejoicing, you go through it together. When there are challenges, you face them together. Where there are memories to be made, you make them together. As great as that reality is, our unity with Christ is even greater than that because after we've walked together through this life, our death will not part us from Him. He's been raised from the dead, never to return to it again and He's promised us eternal life with Him so we can rejoice like the Apostle Paul in the thought that nothing, not even death, can separate us from the love of Christ. His love and our union will never end.

We are cleansed and nourished by Christ

26-27 *That he might sanctify her, having cleansed her by the washing of water with the word, so that he might present the church to himself in splendor, without spot or wrinkle or any such thing, that she might be holy and without blemish.* Christ's love is not aimless. It is a purposeful love. Your purity is His priority. He washed you clean, through the washing of regeneration, the renewal of the Spirit of God. And now He goes on washing you and cleansing you with that effectual word of His that you hold in your hands when you come to worship. This is why the word of God is central in Christian worship. It's how the Bridegroom goes on cleansing His bride, maintaining her purity, nourishing her soul. He does it with His Word.

We are cherished by Christ

28-29 *In the same way husbands should love their wives as their own bodies. He who loves his wife loves himself. For no one ever hated his own flesh, but nourishes and cherishes it, just as Christ does the church.* This means that He sees us and treats us as precious. He watches over us and is jealous over us with a holy jealousy. When was the last time that you were in awe of the fact that God Almighty cherishes you?

We are one with Christ

30-32 *Because we are members of his body. "Therefore a man shall leave his father and mother and hold fast to his wife, and the two shall become one flesh." This mystery is profound, and I am saying that it refers to Christ and the church.* This union defies a comprehensive explanation, and it has a number of implications, but we know that it speaks of the permanency of the relationship that we have with

Him, and the intimacy of that relationship due to the indwelling presence of the Holy Spirit. We don't have to wait for heaven to know what life with Christ will be like, for His Spirit lives with us, even in us, right now!

We are to respect Christ

33 *However, let each one of you love his wife as himself, and let the wife see that she respects her husband.* Isn't it fitting, after He willingly paid our ransom and turned our dark nature and future upside down, that we should joyfully respect the one who so freely loved us?

How our marriages would change if we realized that the relationship that the church has with Jesus Christ is to be mirrored in the relationship that a husband has with his wife, and dedicated ourselves to making it so!

All of these indescribable changes are the result of one thing: God's commitment to redeem us. It was His willingness to pay the price, and His decision to bring us home as His bride, that explain our new identity and our new standing in the world. Could there be a greater rags-to-riches story than the Christian's story? From foreigner to family and from poverty to royalty, all because of what He's done. And one day Jesus will welcome us into His eternal home where we will clearly see Him, and no longer grieve Him, and our time of laboring alone in the fields of this world will be forgotten in the joy of His presence.

9
OVERWHELMED WITH BLESSING
(4:13-22)

As we come to the end of our study of Ruth, we will find that its closing verses are as rich and edifying as we might expect from a book so laden with the fruit of heavenly wisdom. Numerous themes converge in this section, but the truth that binds them all together is that we serve a God who overwhelms us with blessings. Do you ever feel overwhelmed with the blessings of God? If not, then clearly, you aren't paying attention to all that He is doing. Our God is working in innumerable ways to fulfill His eternal purposes for the whole world while showering His people with blessings all around. Winding through this final passage are six streams of blessing flowing from the hand of God Himself, all tied to the blessing of a baby.

Our world really has it all wrong when it comes to children. We're living in a time when children are often looked upon as a burden, a nuisance, an interruption of life and marriage and career, or they are viewed as a source of entertainment. Many people think having a baby is about personal fulfillment and enjoyment. There are myriads of opinions out there that don't match the word of God, but what we want to know is, how does the Bible present children to us? Our search for the answer leads us back to the opening verses of the book.

A Baby is a Gift from God (4:13)

For ten years Ruth and Mahlon were married in Moab. For ten years Orpah and Chilion were married as well. But during that decade not a single child was born to into Naomi's family. This is why she needed a redeemer. This is why Boaz entered the picture, and almost immediately after he did Ruth became pregnant. What's the explanation for this sudden ability to conceive? *The LORD gave her conception.* God's word couldn't be any more clear:

it is the Lord alone who gives life. Whenever a baby is born, that baby is the expression of the handiwork of God that took place in the quietness and secrecy of a mother's womb. Psalm 139:13-16 says: *For you formed my inward parts; you knitted me together in my mother's womb. I praise you, for I am fearfully and wonderfully made. Wonderful are your works; my soul knows it very well. My frame was not hidden from you, when I was being made in secret, intricately woven in the depths of the earth. Your eyes saw my unformed substance; in your book were written, every one of them, the days that were formed for me, when as yet there was none of them.* The emphasis of verse 13 in the Hebrew is on the one doing the action. *You* formed my inward parts; *you* knitted me together. The idea is that God, and God alone, is the author of life. Think about all of the blood vessels, nerves, and countless other strands that run through our bodies. God is the One who knitted all of that together to form a living being. We are not merely the product of biological processes. We were not formed by an impersonal force. So when a baby enters this world and takes its first breath and is placed on the bosom of its mother, I hope we understand what has happened. This is the handiwork of God and a gift of immeasurable value.

A gift for parents

It is God's gift to the union of a husband and a wife. Obed was a gift from God to Boaz and Ruth, and every child is a gift from God to his or her parents and should be treated as such. What are we doing with these precious gifts? Here are some things God says we ought to be doing:

- Ephesians 6:4 *Fathers, do not provoke your children to anger, but bring them up in the discipline and instruction of the Lord.*
- Deuteronomy 6:4-7 *"Hear, O Israel: The LORD our God, the LORD is one. You shall love the LORD your God with all your heart and with all your soul and with all your might. And these words that I command you today shall be on your heart. You shall teach them diligently to your children, and shall talk of them when you sit in your house, and when you walk by the way, and when you lie down, and when you rise.*

The more we recognize that our children are a gift from God, the more we realize that we've been entrusted with a stewardship. These children don't belong to us, not in the truest sense; they belong to the Lord. They've been temporarily placed in our hands that we might raise them in the nurture and admonition of Christ and train them in the love of God. His word instructs us to instruct them in His Word! As we obey, we give evidence that we see our children for what they really are.

A gift for grandparents

What stands out the most in the book of Ruth's conclusion is not Ruth herself. It is the fact that the women speak exclusively to Naomi. The women in this passage saw Obed as a gift from God to Naomi as well. The reason this seems strange to us may be because we have missed the biblical role of grandparents, and therefore we have missed part of God's plan for the family. That's right, the Bible assumes and even assigns a role for grandparents in the lives of their grandchildren! Whenever God gives a picture of a healthy family in His word, and within that context refers to grandparents, they are always portrayed as vitally involved in the lives of their grandchildren.

- Deuteronomy 4:9 *Only take care, and keep your soul diligently, lest you forget the things that your eyes have seen, and lest they depart from your heart all the days of your life. Make them known to your children and your children's children.*

- 2 Timothy 1:5 *I am reminded of your sincere faith, a faith that dwelt first in your grandmother Lois and your mother Eunice and now, I am sure, dwells in you as well.*

- Titus 2:3-5 *Older women likewise are to be reverent in behavior, not slanderers or slaves to much wine. They are to teach what is good, and so train the young women to love their husbands and children, to be self-controlled, pure, working at home, kind, and submissive to their own husbands, that the word of God may not be reviled.*

Most churches love to talk about linking up older women with younger women for training and ministry, and they try to devise all sorts of ministries to do that, and there's nothing wrong with those things. But let us remember that the primary God-ordained way that teaching and instruction is to be passed on is within families. Which means grandmothers teaching their granddaughters how to live a life that brings glory to God.

There are two wrong approaches to avoid when it comes to the role of grandparents in the raising of children. There are many parents who exclude grandparents almost entirely, and that's obviously wrong. There's no doubt that marriage creates a separate family unit. Leaving and cleaving is a God-ordained process which benefits all. It's also true that there can be an unbiblical and ungodly attempt to gain control on the part of grandparents. But it's also wrong when parents decide that they want to cut off all access to their children from the grandparents, thereby preventing those grandparents from exercising their God-ordained responsibilities within the family. Christian parents ought to cherish the wisdom, experience, and lessons that their children gain from interaction with godly grandparents.

Even if the grandparents are unbelievers, there are still valuable things that they can pass on. If nothing else, the love of a grandparent for their grandchildren is something that they will remember with gladness the rest of their lives.

So one wrong approach is to cut off all access to grandparents. The other wrong approach is for grandparents to become selfish. Too selfish to invest in their own progeny, too caught up in their own lives to sacrifice their time for little ones. Believers ought to be elated about the opportunity to have an influence on more than one generation! We've arrived at a sad and selfish place, when we don't want to be involved with that. Thank God that his plans for the family go beyond a single generation. Thank God that no matter how old we get, we never have to separate ourselves from posterity.

A Baby is an Opportunity from God (4:14-16)
Whenever God chooses to give us a child, He hasn't just given us a gift; He has given us an opportunity. In fact, there are at least four opportunities that come with each baby that is born.

An opportunity for new life
Naomi had experienced a lot of heartache through the loss of her husband and two sons. She had no immediate blood relatives left. By the end of chapter one she declares that she has gone from pleasant to bitter: *"do not call me Naomi; call me Mara, for the Almighty has dealt very bitterly with me. I went away full, and the LORD has brought me back empty. Why call me Naomi, when the LORD has testified against me and the Almighty has brought calamity upon me?"* But through the growing relationship of Ruth and Boaz over the course of the last three chapters, we have seen the Lord progressively bringing her back to the pleasantness that had originally characterized her life. And now with the birth of Obed, the journey is complete. This son from God was her opportunity to begin again. He was her opportunity to live again. And there is a sense in which every baby entering the world comes with that same opportunity. You may have had a horrific childhood due to absent or negligent parents, but by God's grace you can be a good and godly mother or father. You may have been a horrible child who brought heartache to your father and mother, but now you can bring joy not only to the heart of your heavenly Father, but also to your mom and dad's heart as they see your responsibility as a parent. You may have failed at raising your own children, but now as a grandparent you can be a righteous influence on the next generation. Every baby can be a *restorer of life*. As parents and grandparents, let's not waste one of the few chances we have for a new lease on life.

An opportunity for new hope

Now Naomi had a *sustainer*. Now she had security because now she had an heir to carry on the name of her dead husband and sons. This grandson would be her loyal protector as she moved into old age. These days it is rarely taught and practiced even less, but children and grandchildren are to be the protectors and providers for their parents when they grow old. We shouldn't have to depend upon the government for our social security when God designed for us to receive it through our family. Psalm 127:4-5 says: *Like arrows in the hand of a warrior are the children of one's youth. Blessed is the man who fills his quiver with them! He shall not be put to shame when he speaks with his enemies in the gate.* Who will stand up for us when we are old against those who assail us in life, if not our grown children? So when a baby is born we are holding the future in our arms, not just the future of the child, but our own future as well!

An opportunity for new relationships

The women of Bethlehem not only recognized the relationship that Naomi would now have with this baby, they also recognized the continuing relationship that Naomi had with her daughter-in-law. The number seven represents completion, so to have seven sons would be equivalent to having a complete home. Yet they declare that this one faithful daughter-in-law, all by herself, was worth more than the two sons she lost, and more than seven more that she could gain. Ruth by herself was enough to make Naomi's home complete. Are you a blessing like that to your parents? What about to your in-laws? Is it possible to overestimate the value of a single godly woman in a family?

This new baby would only serve to strengthen and broaden and deepen the relationship that Naomi and Ruth already had, and it's wonderful to see how the birth of any baby gives new opportunities for relationships to either develop or improve. It tends to bring families together and to open up lines of communication. It opens doors for old hurts and barriers to be put in the past and for new relationships to form.

An opportunity for new love

What exactly is going on when Naomi takes the child in her lap and becomes his nurse? Some have imagined that this is a formal adoption. The idea is that because Boaz was the redeemer whose job was to raise up someone to carry on the name of Elimelech and Mahlon, that he gave this first son Obed to Naomi. In which case Naomi became his legal mother took full responsibility for raising him. The problem with this view is that there is no such process found in Scripture. The Bible never talks about that kind of adoption anywhere. The better way to understand it is to take it literally. What we have here is a grandmother delighting over her first grandchild and taking a prominent role in his upbringing. Don't think of her as a wet nurse, as that would have been impossible, but as filling the role of a modern-day nanny, except that nannies work for pay while Naomi's only reward was the love of Obed. This same Hebrew word אָמַן (*aman*) translated *nurse* is used to describe Mordecai's role as a guardian and nurturer to Esther as well. What a poignant picture this is to see a grandmother dedicate herself to practically loving her grandson instead of taking advantage of her new social status to live selfishly.

What love we've been able to experience because God chose to give us the gift of our children! I'll never forget the birth of our fourth child. My wife and I were having a very hard time financially. I wonder how many people would give the same kind of testimony that at least one of your children was conceived at what seemed like the worst possible moment! Well, that's how it was with our fourth. I will never forget coming home that night. My wife and I were going to sleep. The lights were off. And she said to me, "I went to the doctor today." And I said, "Please don't tell me that you're pregnant." And literally, we didn't speak another word the rest of the night. And I knew exactly what that meant. But after all these years, what would we do without our third son! What would we do without our daughter-in-law whom he married? What would we do without our grandson whom she bore to him? What love we would have missed out on if God had not given us what we were so afraid of!

A Baby Has a Purpose from God (4:17-22)

When Mahlon died in Moab, and this young woman chose to follow her mother-in-law, who would have ever known that she was going to be married to Boaz one day? And who would have ever known that the baby to be born from their union would be the grandfather of King David? And who would have ever known that Naomi and Ruth and Boaz would be in the line of the Messiah? This baby's birth was the farthest thing from an accident. He had a purpose from God, and so does every other child. All of our days are written down before we live one, as we saw earlier from Psalm 139. Every baby has been born into this world for a reason, and one of the greatest and godliest things that a parent can do for a child is to impart to them a sense of purpose. Not a worldly sense of purpose, but a biblical one. They need to know that they're not here by accident, that they were fearfully and wonderfully made, that they're here for a reason. And they need to know that the reason has to do with their relationship with the Lord Jesus Christ. We can help them see that all mankind was created for a definite purpose: to glorify God and to enjoy Him forever.

Why did God form you in the womb? Why did He give you to your parents? Why did He put you on the earth? What is He willing to do with you if you will trust Him? Do you understand there's nothing too difficult for God? Do you understand that the same God who has used both the famous

69

and obscure men and women of history is the God who brought you into this world, and if you trust Him then He can and will use you as well?

I know there will probably be some who read this who desire children but have not been able to have them. Nothing I can write will take away your trial, but I want to comfort you with the thought that children are not the only gift, or even the greatest gift that God gives. After all, we have seen that Ruth was more to Naomi than seven sons. I encourage you to use the freedom of time and resources that you currently have to invest in the Kingdom of God. Raise up spiritual "children" through discipleship, and when God gives you opportunity, you can come alongside parents and grandparents, and have an influence on children as well.

But for those reading this who are parents or grandparents I must ask: Do your thoughts about children align with the things we have learned in this chapter? Do you think about your children or your grandchildren as a gift from God? Do you believe the words of Psalm 127:3 *Behold, children are a heritage from the LORD, the fruit of the womb a reward?* Are you treating them as such? Are you seeing yourself as steward? Are you diligently raising them in the nurture and admonition of the Lord, when they rise up, when they walk through the day, and when they lie down at night? Are you using whatever influence you have to guide them in a Godward direction? Do you realize that with the birth of that baby, God gave you an opportunity? Here is an invitation to new life, to new hope, new relationships and new love. Do you realize that your children or grandchildren were born with a purpose? If not, could it be that you have never discovered your purpose?

Do you realize that you will never know a purposeful life until you know Jesus Christ as your Lord and Savior? Until that day you are bound to live an empty life, a life without meaning, a life defined by groping, searching, and questioning. No matter what else you reach for to satisfy your heart, you'll still be empty. God has given us an entire book of the Bible to teach us that lesson. It's called the Book of Ecclesiastes, and it says *Vanity, vanity, all is vanity*. There was a man in ancient Israel who looked for satisfaction in wealth and women and science and knowledge and power. He had it all, far more than you and I will ever have. And yet he kept saying, *Vanity, vanity, all is vanity*. There was a man in modern America who reached the pinnacle of worldly success only to realize that he had wasted his life to build an "empire of dirt." When will we wise up? When will we listen to the testimony of God and man? When will you put your faith in the only one who is worthy of it?

10
FINAL THOUGHTS

One of the most important questions we can ask about any book of the Bible is, "Why did God see fit to give us this book?" We've looked at the book of Ruth in detail and have found some amazing things. The most amazing is how this true story from thousands of years ago pictures our salvation in Jesus Christ. If we see ourselves accurately and see the Lord accurately, we see that we've been like Elimelech and Naomi, and we've been like Ruth. We've been stubborn. We've been aliens, separated from God's people, in a land of false gods. We've looked for help in the wrong places. We've trusted in our earthly wisdom instead of in the Lord's goodness and the Lord's promises. Yet the Lord has seen fit to call us back home. He's given us useful work to do. He's given us food and water and extra provision and safety. He's redeemed us publicly. He's brought us into his own household, his own family. We, collectively, are the bride of Christ, as Ruth was the bride of Boaz. He's placed his own name upon us, so that we're no longer to be called bitter, but fruitful. He's given us a hope and a future.

Why did the Lord give us the book of Ruth? Surely a main reason is to help us realize the overwhelming blessing that we have in Jesus—and it's all because God chose us before time and predestined us and redeemed us and called us and justified us.

STUDY QUESTIONS –
WHEN GOD LEADS US HOME

Chapter 1 – When Leaving Leads to Loss

1. Re-read the first two sentences, beginning with "There is a time...." Have you ever known such a time in your life?
2. What was the spiritual condition of society like in the days of the book of Ruth?
3. What immediate problem did the people of Bethlehem face? Why should we not be surprised at that?
4. Explain the irony of the names Bethlehem, Elimelech and Naomi.
5. Why was Elimelech's decision to move a sinful decision? (Note that the text gives eight reasons.)
6. Here's a list of the opposites of those reasons. Are they useful in evaluating options for a decision that you currently face?
   a. Remembering your name—Christian
   b. Remembering your identity—child of God
   c. Hanging on to God's commands and promises
   d. Seeing things from a vantage point of faith in God
   e. Majoring on spiritual realities
   f. Giving others a reason to praise God, not to blaspheme Him
   g. Avoiding placing others into temptation
7. What were the sad results of Elimelech's decision?
8. Is the Lord calling you right now to stay in a situation that seems unpleasant or dangerous? Is he calling you to go into a situation that seems unpleasant or dangerous?
9. How can you distinguish between foolishly putting God to the test by taking unnecessary risks, and foolishly avoiding "risks" that he is calling you to take?

Chapter 2 – When God Leads Us Home

1. "Sometimes you cannot move forward until you are willing to go back." Have you seen that in your life?
2. Why was Naomi despondent, even though she made the right decision?
3. What choice did Naomi make on the way home to Bethlehem? What would be possible motivations behind her choice?

4. What choice did Orpah make? Why is it tragic for people to make such a choice? What are they giving up?
5. What choice did Ruth make? What aspects of the choice made it a remarkable choice?
6. How did Naomi feel when she arrived home? How did she describe the changes in her life?
7. Read Hebrews 12:11. How does this relate to Naomi's situation? Have you experienced the truth of this verse?
8. Of these three women, which one's decision is the most like the decisions you've been making lately?

Chapter 3 – The Providence of God

1. In your own words, what is God's providence?
2. What were the duties and privileges of a kinsman-redeemer?
3. What important facts do we learn about Boaz in 2:1-5?
4. What is gleaning? What do the laws about gleaning teach us? Compare and contrast it with the ways we care for the poor today.
5. Have you ever been so poor that you were hungry, or on the edge of hunger? If so, as you look back, can you see any indications of God's providence in the situation?
6. How can you apply the principle of gleaning to your current life situation? Is there anyone for whom you can or should provide an opportunity for "gleaning"—that is, an opportunity to avoid poverty by working?
7. What four aspects of Ruth's character are highlighted by this commentary?
8. Ruth was guided by the Lord, even though she didn't know she was being guided by the Lord. What things had she done (or was she then doing) right, that prepared her for the Lord's guidance?
9. Have you seen the Lord's guidance and provision in remarkable ways in your own life, or maybe in the life of someone else?
10. How will a rock-solid confidence in the Lord's providence change the way you live your life?

Chapter 4 – A Divine Appointment

1. What is Biblical typology?
2. How does a type differ from myth/fable and from an ordinary event that is not a type in the Biblical sense?
3. How do we learn of Boaz' faith in the Lord? How easy is it for people around us to learn of our faith in the Lord?

4. What circumstances did the Lord have to bring together in order for Boaz and Ruth to meet as they did?
5. What circumstances did the Lord have to bring together in order for you to hear the gospel and respond to it?
6. In Boaz' first encounter with Ruth, what things did he do that are admirable?
7. What did Boaz have to gain by his actions toward Ruth?
8. How are Boaz' actions that day toward Ruth a type (a foreshadowing picture) of God's actions toward us?
9. When you look back at your life and the life of your family or church, where do you see the Lord's providence at work?
10. How have you responded to Jesus' offer to be your Kinsman-Redeemer?

Chapter 5 – Living in Hope

1. What is Christian hope? How does it differ from the world's idea of hope?
2. How would Boaz' words and actions have given Ruth hope?
3. Are you now laboring in hope?
4. What are one or two of the ways in which the God has sent you back full?
5. Do you marvel at God's grace to you? If so, do you marvel at His grace seldom or often?
6. How will marveling at God's grace change a person's life?
7. Why is Christian hope humble? Have you seen examples of Christians who have humble hope?
8. What are the reasons why Naomi has hope?
9. How does Ruth respond to Naomi's counsel? Is her response important?

Chapter 6 – A Request for Marriage

1. What factors shape Naomi's plan for Ruth?
2. What did Naomi do in order to put her plan into action?
3. Was it a secret plan? Was it a dishonorable plan? When is a secret plan honorable, and when is it dishonorable?
4. In what ways is Naomi a model for those who are parents or mentors of young single people?
5. What's the difference between trying to look clean, neat and attractive and trying to look sexy and seductive?

6. Imagine yourself in the place of Boaz or of Ruth that night. What would you think or feel?
7. What things did Boaz commend about Ruth? (Is there anything obvious that he did not mention?)
8. What did Boaz promise to do for her?
9. Why did he want to check with the other kinsman before marrying Ruth?
10. What does Boaz' protection of Ruth and his provision for Ruth say to today's men?

Chapter 7 – The Kinsman Redeemer

1. What repeated words or ideas are the theme of chapter 4 of the book of Ruth?
2. Without gossiping, have you ever seen someone use God's sovereignty as an excuse for doing nothing?
3. Where did Boaz go in the morning? Why?
4. What did the other kinsman like about his role as kinsman redeemer? What kept him from fulfilling that role?
5. What did the removal of the sandal indicate?
6. How is Boaz' role in redeeming Ruth like the role of the Lord Jesus Christ in redeeming us? Why is Jesus' humanity important to his work in redeeming people?
7. Lots of churches seldom—if ever—mention the idea of redemption. Why is Jesus' work as a redeemer important? (What do we lose if we lose His redemption?)
8. What things about Ruth make Boaz' choice somewhat surprising?
9. What things about us make Jesus' choice of His bride surprising?

Chapter 8 – The Redeemed Bride

1. What things about a particular wedding might make godly observers rejoice?
2. Review the list concerning the world's view of marriage. What's wrong with these ideas?
3. How is the world's view of marriage different from a fully Christian view of marriage?
4. What are some of the ways that a fully Christian view of marriage will make courtship, a wedding, and a marriage different?
5. What are some ways that you have seen professing Christians either fail or succeed in following the Lord as they marry?

6. Why is it important for both marriage and redemption to be public knowledge?
7. What did the townspeople wish for Boaz and for Ruth?
8. How does human marriage picture the relationship between Christ and the church? If you disobey God's plans for marriage, what are you doing to the picture of Christ and the church?

Chapter 9 – Overwhelmed with Blessing

1. What do most people around you think about children?
2. To see what the world thinks about children, do an internet search for *fertility rate by country*. A fertility rate less than 2 means that the people are not having enough children to replace themselves.
3. What does Psalm 139:13-16 tell us about where we came from?
4. In what way is a baby a gift from God?
5. In what ways is a baby an opportunity?
6. Have you known a baby to bring new life and new hope to a family?
7. Although it's not usually a good idea to assume that a baby will fix every broken relationship, have you known a baby to bring new or repaired or deepened relationships?
8. Do you believe God has a purpose for every child?
9. In your own life and situation, what attitudes or actions concerning babies will most glorify God? Are you willing to trust God's thoughts concerning babies?

ABOUT THE AUTHOR

Richard Caldwell Jr. is the senior pastor at Founders Baptist Church in Spring, Texas. He is married to Jacquelyn, and they have four children and three grandchildren. He has served in pastoral ministry for 33 years, in the roles of youth pastor, church planter, and senior pastor. He is a graduate of Southwestern Baptist Theological Seminary (M.Div.) and The Master's Seminary (D.Min). He is one of seven campus pastors for The Expositor's Seminary, and also serves as a faculty member. Richard's sermons can be heard weekdays on radio (Walking in Grace) in the city of Houston, and on Sermon Audio (http://www.sermonaudio.com).